W9-AZQ-403

CompTIA® Cloud Essentials™ Certification Study Guide

(Exam CLO-001)

ITpreneurs

New York   Chicago   San Francisco
Athens   London   Madrid   Mexico City
Milan   New Delhi   Singapore   Sydney   Toronto

Cataloging-in-Publication Data is on file with the Library of Congress

McGraw-Hill Education books are available at special quantity discounts to use as premiums and sales promotions, or for use in corporate training programs. To contact a representative, please visit the Contact Us pages at www.mhprofessional.com.

CompTIA® Cloud Essentials™ Certification Study Guide (Exam CLO-001)

1234567890   DOC DOC   109876543

ISBN: Book p/n 978-0-07-180040-2 and CD p/n 978-0-07-180042-6
of set 978-0-07-180043-3

MHID: Book p/n 0-07-180040-9 and CD p/n 0-07-180042-5
of set 0-07-180043-3

Sponsoring Editor Meghan Riley Manfre	**Lead Contributor** Daniel Lachance	**Production Supervisor** James Kussow
Editorial Supervisor Jody McKenzie	**Technical Editor** Cazzy Jordan	**Composition** Cenveo Publisher Services
Project Manager Sandhya Gola, Cenveo® Publisher Services	**Copy Editor** Kim Wimpsett	**Illustration** Cenveo Publisher Services
Acquisitions Coordinator Mary Demery	**Proofreader** Paul Tyler	**Art Director, Cover** Jeff Weeks
	Indexer Jack Lewis	**Cover Designer** Peter Grame

Successfully adopting an IT best practice or framework starts with understanding it. **ITpreneurs** develops engaging and effective training materials for professionals to do just that. The materials ensure professionals acquire the knowledge to accelerate careers and grow opportunities in today's dynamic IT environment. ITpreneurs was the first to launch an accredited vendor-neutral cloud course and offers training solutions for more than 14 frameworks. Find out more at ITpreneurs.com.

About the Lead Contributor

Daniel Lachance, CompTIA Cloud Essentials, CompTIA A+, CompTIA Network+, CompTIA Security+, MCT, MCSA, MCITP, MCTS, is a technical trainer for Global Knowledge and has delivered classroom training for a wide variety of products for the past 19 years. He has developed custom applications and planned, implemented, troubleshot, and documented various network configurations. Daniel has worked as a technical editor on a number of certification titles, and he authored *CompTIA Security+ Certification Practice Exams (Exam SY0-301)*.

About the Technical Editor

Cazzy Jordan is responsible for disseminating knowledge for the benefit of organizations looking to leverage and optimize IT investments, people, and processes. As a technologist, with degrees and experience in both psychology and law, Cazzy is able to bring a unique perspective into how organizations and individuals can collaborate and leverage the latest technologies for the benefit of an organization. In his current capacity at General Dynamics, Cazzy engages with clients, partners, end-user organizations, and internal staff to raise awareness of the benefits of cloud computing while also addressing common misconceptions around the cloud. Cazzy was one of the first individuals to obtain the CompTIA Cloud Essentials certification, is a PMP and ITIL Expert, possesses the CompTIA Security+ certification, and is currently working toward a master's in cyber security.

About LearnKey

LearnKey provides self-paced learning content and multimedia delivery solutions to enhance personal skills and business productivity. LearnKey claims the largest library of rich streaming-media training content that engages learners in dynamic media-rich instruction complete with video clips, audio, full-motion graphics, and animated illustrations. LearnKey can be found on the Web at www.LearnKey.com.

CompTIA Approved Quality Content

CompTIA®

It Pays to Get Certified

In a digital world, digital literacy is an essential survival skill. Certification proves you have the knowledge and skill to solve business problems in virtually any business environment. Certifications are highly-valued credentials that qualify you for jobs, increased compensation, and promotion.

LEARN		CERTIFY		WORK
IT is Everywhere	**IT Knowledge and Skills Get Jobs**	**Job Retention**	**New Opportunities**	**High Pay-High Growth Jobs**
IT is mission critical to almost all organizations and its importance is increasing.	Certifications verify your knowledge and skills that qualifies you for:	Competence is noticed and valued in organizations.	Certifications qualify you for new opportunities in your current job or when you want to change careers.	Hiring managers demand the strongest skill set.
• 79% of U.S. businesses report IT is either important or very important to the success of their company	• Jobs in the high growth IT career field • Increased compensation • Challenging assignments and promotions • 60% report that being certified is an employer or job requirement	• Increased knowledge of new or complex technologies • Enhanced productivity • More insightful problem solving • Better project management and communication skills • 47% report being certified helped improve their problem solving skills	• 31% report certification improved their career advancement opportunities	• There is a widening IT skills gap with over 300,000 jobs open • 88% report being certified enhanced their resume

CompTIA Cloud Essentials Certification Advances Your Career

- **Organizations do not have adequate cloud competencies**—especially cloud infrastructure and service providers. Excellent job opportunities exist and will grow for professionals who are knowledgeable about the cloud.
- **The cloud is a new frontier** that requires astute personnel who understand the strategic impact of cloud computing on an organization.
- **The cloud has special security considerations** which business as well as IT staff need to understand.

Steps to Getting Certified and Staying Certified

1. **Review exam objectives.** Review the certification objectives to make sure you know what is covered in the exam: www.comptia.org/certifications/testprep/examobjectives.aspx.

2. **Practice for the exam.** After you have studied for the certification, review and answer sample questions to get an idea of what type of questions might be on the exam, http://certification.comptia.org/samplequestions.aspx.

3. **Purchase an exam voucher.** You can purchase an exam voucher on the CompTIA Marketplace, www.comptiastore.com.

4. **Take the test!** Go to the Pearson VUE website and schedule a time to take your exam, www.pearsonvue.com/comptia/.

Content Seal of Quality

This courseware bears the seal of CompTIA Approved Quality Content. This seal signifies this content covers 100 percent of the exam objectives and implements important instructional design principles. CompTIA recommends multiple learning tools to help increase coverage of the learning objectives.

How to Obtain More Information

- ■ **Visit CompTIA online** Go to http://certification.comptia.org/home.aspx to learn more about getting CompTIA certified.
- ■ **Contact CompTIA** Please call 866-835-8020 and choose option 2 or e-mail questions@comptia.org.
- ■ **Connect with CompTIA** Find us on Facebook, LinkedIn, Twitter, and YouTube.

CAQC Disclaimer

The logo of the CompTIA Approved Quality Content (CAQC) program and the status of this or other training material as "Approved" under the CompTIA Approved Quality Content program signifies that, in CompTIA's opinion, such training material covers the content of CompTIA's related certification exam.

The contents of this training material were created for the CompTIA Cloud Essentials exam covering CompTIA certification objectives that were current as of the date of publication.

CompTIA has not reviewed or approved the accuracy of the contents of this training material and specifically disclaims any warranties of merchantability or fitness for a particular purpose. CompTIA makes no guarantee concerning the success of persons using any such "Approved" or other training material in order to prepare for any CompTIA certification exam.

CONTENTS AT A GLANCE

CONTENTS

PREFACE

The objective of this study guide is to prepare you for the CompTIA Cloud Essentials exam by familiarizing you with the characteristics of cloud computing, related technologies, and how cloud adoption provides business value. Because the primary focus of the book is to help you pass the test, we don't always cover every aspect of the related technology. Some aspects of the technology are covered only to the extent necessary to help you understand what you need to know to pass the exam, but we hope this book will serve you as a valuable professional resource after your exam.

In This Book

This book is organized in such a way as to serve as an in-depth review for the CompTIA Cloud Essentials exam for IT and project management professionals. Each chapter covers a major aspect of the exam, with an emphasis on the "why" as well as the "how to" of working with and supporting cloud adoption and governance.

Exam Readiness Checklist

At the end of the introduction you will find an Exam Readiness Checklist. This checklist has been constructed to allow you to cross-reference the official exam objectives with the objectives as they are presented and covered in this book. This checklist also allows you to gauge your level of expertise with each objective at the outset of your studies. This will allow you to check your progress and ensure you spend the time you need on more difficult or unfamiliar sections. The objectives are listed as presented by the certifying body with the corresponding section of this study guide that covers that objective and a chapter and page reference.

In Every Chapter

We've created a set of chapter components that call your attention to important items, reinforce important points, and provide helpful exam-taking hints. Take a look at what you'll find in every chapter:

- Every chapter begins with **Certification Objectives**—what you need to know in order to pass the section on the exam dealing with the chapter topic. The "Certification Objective" headings identify the objectives within the chapter, so you'll always know an objective when you see it!

- **Exam Watch** notes call attention to information about, and potential pitfalls in, the exam.

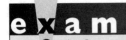

The operative phrase to watch for on the exam is "exclusive use."   *Questions using this phrase are most likely referring to a private cloud solution.*

- **On the Job** notes describe the issues that come up most often in real-world settings. They provide a valuable perspective on certification- and product-related topics. They point out common mistakes and address questions that have arisen from on-the-job discussions and experience.

- The **Certification Summary** is a succinct review of the chapter and a restatement of salient points regarding the exam.

✓ - The **Two-Minute Drill** at the end of every chapter is a checklist of the main points of the chapter. You can use it for last-minute review.

Q&A - The **Self Test** offers questions similar to those found on the exam. The answers to these questions, as well as explanations of the answers, can be found at the end of each chapter. By taking the Self Test after completing each chapter, you'll reinforce what you've learned from that chapter while becoming familiar with the structure of the exam questions.

Electronic Practice Exams

Accompanying this book are two practice exams each consisting of 50 questions. The practice exam that is included on this book's CD-ROM is also included as Appendix B at the back of this book. A second practice exam is available for download. To register for this second practice exam, click the Bonus MasterExam link on the CD-ROM's main launch page and follow the directions for free online registration.

You won't see the same questions on the practice exams as will appear on the real CLO-001 exam, but the question format, style, and content will help you prepare. Do not attempt the practice exams until you have read and understood each chapter in this book.

Some Pointers

Once you've finished reading this book, set aside some time to do a thorough review. You might want to return to the book several times and make use of all the methods it offers for reviewing the material.

1. **Reread all the Two-Minute Drills,** or have someone quiz you. You also can use the drills as a way to do a quick cram before the exam. You may want to make flashcards out of 3 × 5 index cards with the Two-Minute Drill material.

2. **Reread all the Exam Watch notes**. Remember that these notes are written by those who have taken the exam and passed. They know what you should expect—and what you should be on the lookout for.

3. **Retake the Self Tests**. Taking the tests right after you've read the chapter is a good idea because the questions help reinforce what you've just learned. However, it's an even better idea to go back later and answer all the questions in the book in a single sitting. Pretend you're taking the live exam. When you go through the questions the first time, you should mark your answers on a separate piece of paper. That way, you can run through the questions as many times as you need to until you feel comfortable with the material.

INTRODUCTION

The CompTIA Cloud Essentials exam is a vendor-neutral exam testing your knowledge of various cloud computing models, their risks, how they provide business value, how to move to cloud services, and how those services can be effectively managed. This certification is designed for IT professionals, business analysts, service provider or data center personnel, and project managers. CompTIA recommends individuals seeking this certification have six months of experience working in an environment that markets or relies on IT-related services. There is no expiration of this CompTIA certification as of this writing.

Exam Structure

On the CompTIA Cloud Essentials exam you can expect to see multiple-choice questions. While most questions will have a single correct answer, you will get the occasional question asking you to select two correct answers or all correct answers. Unlike some vendor certification exams, there are no scenario-based questions with the Cloud Essentials exam; each question is independent of others.

There are six domains, or major topic areas, that you can expect to be tested on. These domains and their percentage of the exam are as follows:

1.0	Characteristics of Cloud Services From a Business Perspective	15 percent
2.0	Cloud Computing and Business Value	20 percent
3.0	Technical Perspectives/Cloud Types	20 percent
4.0	Steps to Successful Adoption of Cloud Computing	15 percent
5.0	Impact and Changes of Cloud Computing on IT Service Management	15 percent
6.0	Risks and Consequences of Cloud Computing	15 percent

The following table provides further exam information:

Exam Details	
Number of questions	50
Length of test	60 minutes
Passing score	720
Languages	English, Japanese, and Portuguese
Exam code	CLO-001

The passing score is 720 on a scale of 900.

Registering for the Exam

Once you have read and understood this study guide and completed both included practice exams, you can sign up for the exam through Pearson VUE testing centers at www.pearsonvue.com. If this is your first time registering for an exam online with Pearson VUE, you will have to create a free account. Once signed in with the account, you can select a date and time at the closest testing center giving the CompTIA Cloud Essentials CLO-001 exam. The cost of the exam, at the time of this writing, is $191 USD. If you are taking this exam because of a business requirement, check whether your employer has exam vouchers or whether you will be reimbursed after taking the exam. The Pearson VUE site does provide receipts of exam payments, as well as proof of passing the exam.

Bring two pieces of identification with you to the testing center (one must be a photo ID). If you forget, you will not be allowed to take the exam. Arrive at least 15 minutes early for your appointment. You are not allowed to bring smartphones or any other type of device or paper into the examination room. Pearson VUE testing centers have secure locations where testers can keep their jackets, smartphones, and so on, while they are being tested.

Taking the Exam

Get a full night's sleep each night leading up to your exam. Staying up late cramming right up to the exam day is a bad idea; plan a study schedule to ensure you have time to properly prepare.

Read each question carefully and ask yourself "What am I being asked?" In some cases, every possible answer may look correct, so be sure you understand what is being asked. You might consider eliminating answers that you know are incorrect as you think of the correct answer. Note that the points are not deducted for incorrect answers, so you should attempt every question. Immediately after completing your exam, your testing computer screen will indicate whether you passed.

Good luck!

Exam CLO-001

Exam Readiness Checklist

Official Objective	Study Guide Coverage	Ch. No.	Pg. No.	Beginner	Intermediate	Expert
1.0 Characteristics of Cloud Services From a Business Perspective						
1.1 Understand common terms and definitions of cloud computing and provide examples	Cloud Computing: Common Terms and Definitions	1	2			
1.2 Describe the relationship between cloud computing and virtualization	Cloud Computing and Virtualization	1	5			
1.3 Name early examples of cloud computing	Early Examples of Cloud Computing	1	6			
1. 4 Understand several common definitions of cloud computing and their commonalities/differences	Cloud Computing: Common Terms and Definitions	1	2			
1.5 Recognize what types of organizations might benefit from cloud computing	Positive Indicators for Cloud Readiness	1	9			
1.6 Recognize what type of organizations might not benefit from cloud computing	Negative Indicators for Cloud Readiness	1	10			
1.7 Distinguish between the different types of clouds, including XaaS, IaaS, PaaS, and give examples of them	Cloud Service Categories	1	11			
2.0 Cloud Computing and Business Value						
2.1 Recognize the similarities and differences between cloud computing and outsourcing	Similarities and Differences Between Cloud Computing and Outsourcing	2	24			

Exam Readiness Checklist

Official Objective	Study Guide Coverage	Ch. No.	Pg. No.	Beginner	Intermediate	Expert
2.2 Understand the following characteristics of clouds and cloud services from a business perspective: ■ Scalability ■ Security ■ Hardware independence ■ Variable costs ■ Time to market ■ Distribution over the Internet	Characteristics of Clouds and Cloud Services from a Business Perspective	2	27			
2.3 Demonstrate how the characteristics of cloud computing enhance business value	How the Characteristics of Cloud Computing Enhance Business Value	2	30			
3.0 Technical Perspectives/Cloud Types						
3.1 Understand the differences between private and public types of clouds from a technical perspective and provide examples	Differences Between Public and Private Clouds	3	42			
3.2 Understand at a high level the following important techniques and methods for cloud computing deployment: ■ Networking ■ Automation and Self Service ■ Federation ■ The role of standardization	Techniques and Methods for Cloud Computing Deployment	3	51			

Exam Readiness Checklist

Exam Readiness Checklist

Official Objective	Study Guide Coverage	Ch. No.	Pg. No.	Beginner	Intermediate	Expert
4.4 Describe multiple approaches for migrating applications	Migrating Applications to the Cloud	4	80			
5.0 Impact and Changes of Cloud Computing on IT Service Management						
5.1 Understand the impact and changes cloud computing has on IT service management in a typical organization	Cloud Computing Changes on IT Service Managment	5	92			
5.2 Use a structured approach based on ITIL to explore the potential impact of cloud computing in your organization	Explore the Potential Impact of Cloud Computing Using ITIL	5	96			
6.0 Risks and Consequences of Cloud Computing						
6.1 Explain and identify the issues associated with integrating cloud computing into an organization's existing compliance risk and regulatory framework: Security Legal, Compliance, Privacy risks	Identify Challenges in Integrating Cloud Computing into an Organization's Existing Governance Framework	6	108			
6.2 Explain the implications for direct cost and cost allocations	Explain the Implications for Direct Cost and Cost Allocations	6	113			
6.3 Understand how to maintain strategic flexibility	Understand How to Maintain Strategic Flexibility	6	115			

1

Introduction to
Cloud Computing

Over the past few years, virtualization and cloud computing have changed the way information technology (IT) is organized. It has become less important for companies to maintain their own local servers and more advantageous for them to share computing resources, which may be owned by a third-party service provider. Virtualization enables hardware to be shared among virtual servers. Cloud computing enables these servers to be shared with multiple users so that their location does not matter anymore, as shown in Figure 1-1.

Cloud Computing: Common Terms and Definitions

Figure 1-2 illustrates that cloud computing is a business model using old technology (virtualization, servers, and disk storage) where ownership of physical resources rests with one party and where the service users are billed for their real use. An organization can even use virtualization for internal customers, or an organization can subscribe to cloud services over the Internet.

Cloud computing means different things to different types of people. An IT administrator might define it as the sharing of pooled computing resources over the Internet. A business owner could refer to cloud computing as using software that is hosted on a cloud provider's equipment, which could result in a cost advantage compared to hosting these services internally. A home user might refer to cloud computing in terms of the free storage of files at a cloud provider's site as opposed to storing files locally on a personal device.

All of these definitions share common characteristics, including the use of offsite hosted computing services accessible over a network, such as the Internet. However, these definitions differ in terms of what types of computing services are offered and

---

FIGURE 1-1

With cloud computing, location is not relevant.

Cloud Computing

Location – Inconsequential!

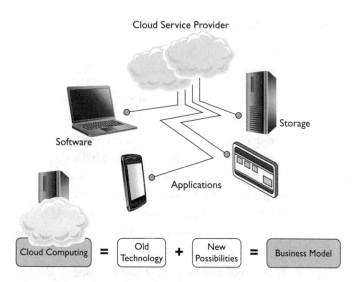

FIGURE 1-2

Cloud computing is a business model using old technology.

at what cost. Public cloud computing refers to IT services being offered to any user with an Internet connection, whereas private cloud computing refers to IT services being offered within a single organization on that organization's equipment.

With cloud computing, the cloud service provider hosts and gives access to the software and data storage. Data might be stored in one or more data centers and might even be replicated between data centers for data redundancy.

Existing technologies such as *virtualization* allows multiple computer operating systems (virtual servers, or cloud servers) to run simultaneously on one physical computer as if they were each running on their own dedicated computer.

There are distinct categories of cloud computing services. *Platform as a Service* (PaaS) allows developers to create and test software without the investment in expensive in-house hardware. *Software as a Service* (SaaS) answers desktop productivity needs for end users. *Infrastructure as a Service* (IaaS) allows IT operations personnel to run applications in the cloud instead of using in-house computing equipment.

As organizations grow or shrink, they can simply request more (or less) computing resources from their provider and pay the corresponding fee. This ability to rapidly add and remove computing resources is called *elasticity*. For paid cloud services, in addition to a monthly subscription fee, you would pay usage fees. For example, the more disk space you use to store files in the cloud, the more you would pay. This means capacity planning is an important skill since it can save organizations money.

Types of computing resources a client could consume include the following:

- Email accounts
- Data storage
- Data backup

- Servers (virtual machines)
- Customized websites

Cloud Computing Characteristics

The National Institute of Standards and Technology (NIST) states that cloud computing services have the following attributes, as shown in Figure 1-3:

- **Elasticity** You can add or remove services/users quickly. This allows an organization to grow or shrink on demand as there are spikes in business activity.

- **On-demand** You can access the service from anywhere, anytime, often simply using a web browser. The physical location of the software and your data at any given time is not known and may be spread across multiple data centers; this maximizes the "anywhere, anytime" nature of cloud computing.

- **Pooled computing resources at the provider's site** The provider invests in the proper hardware, configuration, maintenance, and auditing of their physical infrastructure.

- **Monitored and measured service usage** Paid cloud services often have a monthly recurring subscription fee as well as usage fees. Time using a specific resource, percentage of processing capabilities, amount of disk space used—these are all monitored by the cloud provider that then charges customers accordingly.

- **Broad network access** Access to cloud services is available from any type of computing device such as a smartphone, table, laptop, or desktop computer over the Internet.

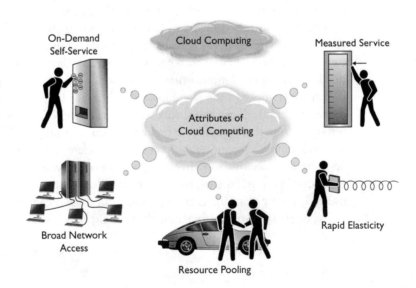

FIGURE 1-3

Cloud computing characteristics

Cloud elasticity is similar to scalability. Whereas scalability is defined as the ability of a system to grow to accommodate need, elasticity *allows cloud customers to not only increase but also decrease the amount of IT services consumed.*

CERTIFICATION OBJECTIVE 1.02

Cloud Computing and Virtualization

Virtualization technology makes cloud computing possible, and it has been around for decades. Providers can host many virtual machines based on client needs without allocating a physical server to each client. Some cloud offerings do allow clients to use physical servers, but this is costly and is not a common approach.

Nonvirtualized computers have one set of hardware and one set of software, as shown in Figure 1-4. Virtualization is a set of techniques for hiding hardware resources behind software abstractions to simplify the way in which other software or end users interact with those resources.

The popular press typically identifies virtualization as a category of vendor products. However, in an enterprise, virtualization should be understood as an integrated approach encompassing software, hardware, and a number of techniques and processes that, when taken together, increase the ease with which IT assets can be delivered, managed, and shared.

Besides creating cloud virtual servers on demand, you can even migrate a physical or virtual on-premises server in your organization to the cloud. This allows for a quicker and smoother transition to cloud-delivered services.

FIGURE 1-4

Multiple virtual machines run on a single virtualization host.

Virtual Environment

CERTIFICATION OBJECTIVE 1.03

Early Examples of Cloud Computing

The swinging 1960s introduced the concept of what we now know as cloud computing. Computing resources were so expensive during that era that time sharing became a common means of allowing different groups of people to use computing power concurrently by doing their work in isolated sessions. Government agencies, universities, and some private organizations were part of this. Cloud computing does not have to be available to public subscribers; *private clouds* offer computing access within an organization.

In the 1990s Hotmail was (and still is!) widely used as a *public cloud* service to access email from a web browser instead of a specific mail program. This meant you could access your email from any Internet-connected machine without having to install and configure specific mail software. *Application service providers* (ASPs) at this time offered additional services beyond email that were available to users through a web browser. ASPs differ from cloud services in that clients purchased specific software to be hosted by the ASP. The problem with this approach was that providers did not have expertise in the wide array of hosted software used by their clients. With cloud services, providers offer standard software to their clients, such as Hotmail or Google Docs; these both are examples of Software as a Service.

INSIDE THE EXAM

Don't get too caught up in technical details for the Cloud Essentials exam. Much of what you will be asked applies to making decisions that relate to business needs. This includes saving money while not sacrificing performance, security, and reliability.

However, knowing the correct meaning for terminology and acronyms will go a long way toward ensuring your success, so keep reading!

CERTIFICATION OBJECTIVE 1.04

Cloud Computing Deployment Models

As we have seen, cloud computing can be available to any subscriber or just within an organization. In addition to the cloud service models, there are also a number of ways to deliver or roll out these cloud services. In some of these deployment models, the financial commitment lies with the organizations that use these clouds. This means they do not completely fit our earlier definitions of cloud computing.

- Private cloud
- Community cloud
- Public cloud
- Hybrid cloud

Figure 1-5 depicts the ways in which these cloud services can be deployed.

Private Cloud

Companies using their own hardware and software assets to deliver web services are said to be using a *private cloud*. This solution will usually use virtualization and may offer a web portal that allows managers to provision services for their users.

FIGURE 1-5

Cloud deployment models

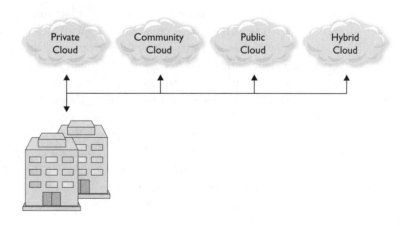

Community Cloud

Community clouds pool computing resources and make them available to several organizations with common needs, such as very quick access time to an application or adherence to strict security and audit guidelines. Cloud customers are often referred to as *tenants*. *Multitenancy* often describes the multiple cloud customers using a shared pool of computing resources. Even if cloud customers are using the same cloud services, each customer must have an isolated computing environment from other cloud customers where their configurations and data are stored separately.

Public Cloud

Public clouds offer computing services to all Internet users. This is what most people think of when they think of cloud computing. Some cloud offerings are free, such as Gmail and Google Docs. Others, such as Microsoft Office 365, require that customers pay a subscription and usage fee for services delivered via their Internet connection. The service provider has made the investment in computing resources, and this frees up capital resources for enterprise customers.

An Internet connection is required for public cloud subscribers. The nature of the cloud service and how many local users will access it concurrently can sometimes necessitate a better Internet link. The amount of data throughput, often expressed in bits per second (bps), is referred to as *bandwidth*. A 100 megabit per second (100Mbps) connection allows more throughput than a 20Mbps connection.

Hybrid Cloud

Hybrid clouds are a combination of both public and private clouds. An organization can integrate some of their on-premises services with a cloud provider. For example, a company's local user accounts can be used to authenticate against cloud services such as cloud email and cloud storage. Authenticating users in one environment and authorizing them to use resources in a different environment is referred to as *federation*, which is discussed in further detail in Chapter 3.

A second hybrid cloud example might include a company with an on-premises email server that uses a cloud antivirus service. Of course, this would imply a trusted network connection between the mail server and the cloud provider.

Cloud computing appeals to business leaders because it is a business concept; in other words, you pay only for what you use ("pay as you go" or "rent instead of buy"). From a business or financial perspective, this could be interpreted as meaning computing dollars can be categorized as operating costs rather than capital expenditures. Accountants and business leaders will not be interested in the underlying virtualization technology that makes this all possible. Chapter 3 discusses public and private cloud deployment models in more detail.

CERTIFICATION OBJECTIVE 1.05

Positive Indicators for Cloud Readiness

Buying hardware, buying software licenses, paying IT staff to install and support the hardware and software—these all require capital that might be put to better use elsewhere within an organization. For small and new businesses, the capital to invest in IT might be nonexistent. Paying only for what you use can be an affordable solution to meet your computing needs, and this applies equally to larger enterprises. Virtualization and cloud computing can overcome the following problems:

- Running out of capacity
- Costly excess capacity
- Tied-up capital

Figure 1-6 shows the problems that can be solved with the proper cloud solution. Businesses that grow or shrink rapidly benefit greatly from elasticity. Sometimes projects undertaken by a business require an IT investment only until project completion. Why have expensive computer hardware and software sit idle at the end of a project? Cloud services can grow and shrink as your business needs do, and

FIGURE 1-6

Problems overcome by using cloud computing

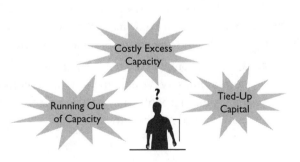

you pay only for what you are using. Think of your water bill; you pay only for the amount of water you've used.

Netflix presents a great example of elastic infrastructure needs. Media content must be converted to many different formats since there are so many different viewing devices. Even though Netflix is Internet content delivered to the end user (otherwise known as Software as a Service), Netflix requires enormous processing and storage capabilities (also known as Infrastructure as a Service). Once the media conversion is complete, the usage charges for CPU utilization cease. Compare this to Netflix purchasing all of the hardware required for periodic media conversions.

on the **job**

One of the most common cloud computing concerns is data security. Cloud providers must pass periodic third-party audits, and as such your data is probably safer with them than with you. Despite this, many decision makers consider this a showstopper.

CERTIFICATION OBJECTIVE 1.06

Negative Indicators for Cloud Readiness

Not all organizations benefit from virtualization and public cloud computing.

- Predictable and fixed workloads can typically make optimal use of their hardware and do not need the scaling.
- Organizations that own large data centers often have enough scale to be as flexible and efficient as cloud computing providers are. They will, however, typically benefit from virtualizing their infrastructure.
- Legal and security reasons, also termed *compliance reasons*, can require an organization to know more details about the location of its data and servers than a cloud computing provider can provide.
- Organizations with systems requiring a high degree of operational assurance, such as military systems and systems responsible for health, safety, and emergency response, may be a poor fit for the guarantees offered by typical public cloud service providers today.

FIGURE I-7

Cloud computing is not always the best choice.

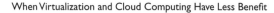

When Virtualization and Cloud Computing Have Less Benefit

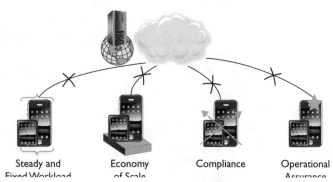

| Steady and Fixed Workload | Economy of Scale | Compliance | Operational Assurance |

Cloud computing is not a cookie-cutter solution to all financial and technology challenges an organization may face, as shown in Figure 1-7. Care must be taken when evaluating potential cloud solutions.

As mentioned, essential services such as emergency, health, law enforcement, or the military may not be suitable cloud customers. Cloud providers provide *service level agreements* (SLAs) to their clients. SLAs guarantee clients a certain level of service and uptime, but this may not be acceptable to the essential services listed earlier.

CERTIFICATION OBJECTIVE 1.07

Cloud Service Categories

Cloud usage models have evolved over time as a result of user needs. What follows are the three most common cloud service categories, also listed in Figure 1-8.

■ **Software as a Service (SaaS)**   For users. A user account allows access to software that is accessible anytime from anywhere using a web browser. Data is stored in the cloud and thus facilitates collaboration. Examples include Gmail, Salesforce, and LinkedIn.

■ **Platform as a Service (PaaS)**   For developers. This service model allows rapid development of new applications and websites. Servers, networking, storage, databases, and so on, are made available by the cloud provider. Vendor-specific

Cloud computing
models

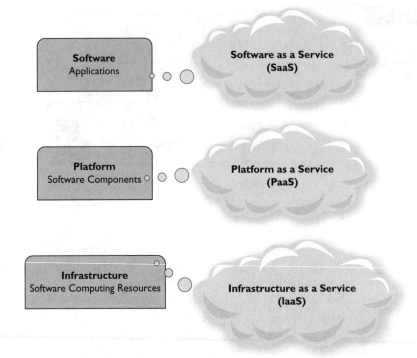

tools present the issue of vendor lock-in. Examples include Windows Azure and
Google App Engine.

■ **Infrastructure as a Service (IaaS)** For IT administrators. Infrastructure
includes the self-provisioning of servers, storage, and so on, via a web-based
portal. This service model includes the creation of cloud servers, cloud-based
storage, and backup. Examples include Rackspace and Amazon S3 Storage.
Companies using some of these services include Shell, the *New York Times*,
and NASDAQ.

Anything as a Service (XaaS) is a term for any service delivered over the Internet
instead of being hosted locally on your network, so it includes IaaS, PaaS, SaaS, and
many others.

on the
job *There are many other classifications of cloud services such as Disaster
Recovery as a Service (DRaaS), Desktop as a Service (DaaS), and many more.*

CERTIFICATION SUMMARY

This chapter defined cloud computing terms and provided examples illustrating their meaning. We discussed the meaning of terms such as *elasticity*, as well as how cloud services allow subscribers to pay only for services they use.

We then canvassed how virtualization makes cloud services possible. The cloud user may not even be aware that virtualized servers are hosting the services they use (SaaS), where other times the administrator creates their own virtual machines (IaaS).

Just like virtualization, we learned that cloud computing is not a new, cutting-edge technology. Time-sharing on expensive computer equipment in the 1960s paved the way for shared resource usage today with cloud computing.

Where virtualization is the enabling technology, cloud computing is a business concept. It sometimes makes business sense to allocate funds as operational costs (cloud computing) versus capital expenditures (locally hosted applications).

We then weighed the benefits and disadvantages of cloud solutions for differing organizations. Those with relatively unchanging IT workload demands and number of employees might not benefit from the cloud. Because cloud services can scale quickly, they make sense for businesses that grow and shrink and for businesses not interested or able to tie up capital in computer-related costs.

Finally, we identified types of cloud services and gave examples of each.

✓ TWO-MINUTE DRILL

Cloud Computing: Common Terms and Definitions

❑ Cloud services are hosted on hardware at another location, and as such, the hardware is somebody else's responsibility.

❑ Cloud services are accessible on demand from any device using a web browser and an Internet connection.

❑ Elasticity allows you to add or remove cloud services or user accounts at any time.

❑ Virtualization allows multiple installed operating systems to run simultaneously on a single computer system.

Cloud Computing and Virtualization

❑ Virtualization hides the details related to physical hardware from a virtual machine.

❑ Virtualization is a technology, whereas cloud computing is a business model.

❑ Cloud computing can use self-provisioning web portals where administrators can create their own virtual machines in the cloud.

❑ An existing physical or virtual server in an organization can be migrated to the cloud to save configuration time.

Early Examples of Cloud Computing

❑ Time-sharing on expensive mainframe computers stems from the 1960s and was the first form of shared resource pooling.

❑ The 1980s and 1990s saw application service providers (ASPs) offering hosted solutions.

❑ Cloud services differ from ASPs in that clients don't buy software and provide it to ASPs for hosting; cloud clients simply pay to use software already offered by the provider.

Cloud Computing Deployment Models

❑ Cloud computing is a business concept where software is delivered to clients over the Internet, so there is minimal local hardware and software to maintain.

❑ Private clouds are designed within a specific organization.

❑ Community clouds are designed for multiple organizations sharing the same computing needs.

❑ Public clouds are available to any public subscriber on the Internet.

❑ Hybrid clouds combine a company's local private cloud with a provider's public cloud, often for authentication purposes.

Positive Indicators for Cloud Readiness

❑ Because of elasticity, cloud services are best suited for businesses that grow and shrink often or whose IT workloads are unpredictable.

❑ Investing in local hardware, software, and licensing, as well as IT support, can be costly; most of this gets shifted to the cloud provider.

❑ Similar to utilities such as water and electricity, with cloud computing you pay only for the services you use.

Negative Indicators for Cloud Readiness

❑ Predictable workloads better utilize costly computer hardware.

❑ Companies that do not grow or shrink dynamically do not need to scale their computer resource usage.

❑ Legal or regulatory requirements might disallow the use of cloud resources.

❑ Cloud reliability may not be enough for mission-critical systems related to law enforcement, military, or emergency services.

Cloud Service Categories

❑ Anything as a Service (XaaS) is a generic term for any computing service delivered over a network.

❑ Software as a Service (SaaS) is for end users and delivers a web app over the Internet to a user using a web browser.

❑ Platform as a Service (Paas) is for software developers and allows the use of virtual machine environments with specific development environments and back-end databases.

❑ Infrastructure as a Service (Iaas) is for IT administrators and includes cloud servers, cloud storage, cloud backup, and so on.

SELF TEST

The following questions will help you measure your understanding of the material presented in this chapter. Read all the choices carefully because there might be more than one correct answer.

Cloud Computing: Common Terms and Definitions

1. With cloud computing services, hardware purchases, software purchases, and IT support are the responsibility of whom?
   A. Internet service provider
   B. RraaS provider
   C. SaaS provider
   D. Application service provider

2. Which term best describes the ability to rapidly increase user accounts for a given cloud service?
   A. Volatility
   B. Synchronicity
   C. Viability
   D. Elasticity

Cloud Computing and Virtualization

3. Which option describes a benefit of virtualized servers?
   A. Shared hardware
   B. Individual hardware per virtual server
   C. Physical servers taking less room space than virtual servers
   D. Virtual servers taking less disk space than physical servers

4. Your company runs a virtualized web application server in-house. You decide to make the web applications available over the Internet through a cloud provider. Which method represents the quickest way to accomplish this?
   A. Create a new cloud server, install web services, and install and configure web applications.
   B. Create a new cloud server, install web services, and import web application data.
   C. Migrate your in-house web application server to the cloud.
   D. This cannot be done—only generic applications are available through the cloud.

Early Examples of Cloud Computing

5. Which term from the past describes the sharing of mainframe computing resources?
   A. Time-sharing
   B. Time division multiplexing
   C. Mainframe-sharing
   D. XaaS

6. Purchasing software and providing it to a third party that installs and manages that software is an example of which of the following?
   A. Virtualization
   B. Application service provider
   C. Platform as a service
   D. Private cloud

Cloud Computing Deployment Models

7. You are the IT director for a retail clothing outlet. Your competitors are using Internet-delivered inventory, storage, and backup solutions from a specific provider. You conclude it is best that your company use the same services from the same provider. What type of cloud will you be subscribing to?
   A. Community cloud
   B. Retail cloud
   C. Private cloud
   D. Public cloud

Positive Indicators for Cloud Readiness

8. For which businesses would cloud computing be best suited? (Choose two.)
   A. Waterfront marketplace that thrives during the summer tourist season
   B. Rural medical practice with four employees
   C. Law enforcement agency
   D. A new company start-up that manufactures watercraft

Negative Indicators for Cloud Readiness

9. Which of the following are valid reasons for not adopting a cloud solution? (Choose two.)
   A. Local hardware is being fully utilized for unchanging IT workloads.
   B. The number of employees rarely changes.
   C. The number of employees changes often.
   D. A business experiences unpredictable project spikes throughout the year.

Cloud Service Categories

10. As a developer for a software company, you have decided to build and test your web applications in a cloud environment. Which type of cloud service best meets your needs?
    A. PaaS
    B. SaaS
    C. IaaS
    D. XaaS

SELF TEST ANSWERS

Cloud Computing: Common Terms and Definitions

1. With cloud computing services, hardware purchases, software purchases, and IT support are the responsibility of whom?
   A. Internet service provider
   B. RraaS provider
   C. SaaS provider
   D. Application service provider

   ☑ **C.** Software as a Service (SaaS) providers deliver web-based software over an Internet connection. The user requires only a machine with a web browser to connect. The cloud providers must supply the hardware and software to deliver the service over the Internet.
   ☒ **A** is incorrect. Internet service providers present us with a connection to the Internet but not cloud services. **B** is incorrect. RraaS is not a valid acronym that relates to cloud computing. **D** is incorrect because application service providers (ASPs) are not the same as cloud providers; ASPs host software that you provide to them.

2. Which term best describes the ability to rapidly increase user accounts for a given cloud service?
   A. Volatility
   B. Synchronicity
   C. Viability
   D. Elasticity

   ☑ **D.** Elasticity allows consumer of cloud services to quickly add or remove user accounts.
   ☒ **A, B,** and **C** are incorrect because these terms are not related to rapidly adding user accounts related to a cloud service.

Cloud Computing and Virtualization

3. Which option describes a benefit of virtualized servers?
   A. Shared hardware
   B. Individual hardware per virtual server
   C. Physical servers taking less room space than virtual servers
   D. Virtual servers taking less disk space than physical servers

☑ **A.** A single physical server can host multiple virtual machines so that the hardware is shared by the virtual machines.

☒ **B, C,** and **D** are incorrect. Virtual servers do not each have their own hardware; they share the physical hardware of the virtualization host. Physical servers take much more physical room space than virtual servers, of which there could be many running on a single physical server. Disk space varies depending on the role of the server, whether it is physical or virtual.

4. Your company runs a virtualized web application server in-house. You decide to make the web applications available over the Internet through a cloud provider. Which method represents the quickest way to accomplish this?

A. Create a new cloud server, install web services, and install and configure web applications.

B. Create a new cloud server, install web services, and import web application data.

C. Migrate your in-house web application server to the cloud.

D. This cannot be done—only generic applications are available through the cloud.

☑ **C.** Since the in-house server is already virtualized, it is quicker to simply migrate it to the cloud as a cloud server.

☒ **A** and **B** are incorrect because they both involve the creation of the web application server from scratch—this is not a quick method. **D** is incorrect because the cloud offers much more than simply generic web apps.

Early Examples of Cloud Computing

5. Which term from the past describes the sharing of mainframe computing resources?

A. Time-sharing

B. Time division multiplexing

C. Mainframe-sharing

D. XaaS

☑ **A.** Time-sharing allowed groups of people to use expensive mainframe computing resources concurrently by working in isolated computing sessions.

☒ **B** is incorrect because time division multiplexing is a signal transmission protocol. **C** is not an industry-accepted term. **D** refers to any web service delivered over the Internet (Anything as a Service) and thus is incorrect.

6. Purchasing software and providing it to a third party that installs and manages that software is an example of which of the following?
   A. Virtualization
   B. Application service provider
   C. Platform as a service
   D. Private cloud

   ☑ **B.** Application service providers (ASPs) host software that their client provides.
   ☒ **A, C,** and **D** are incorrect. Virtualization uses physical hardware to run multiple virtual machines. Platform as a Service is a cloud solution for software developers. Private clouds deliver services over networks to private organizations.

Cloud Computing Deployment Models

7. You are the IT director for a retail clothing outlet. Your competitors are using Internet-delivered inventory, storage, and backup solutions from a specific provider. You conclude it is best that your company use the same services from the same provider. What type of cloud will you be subscribing to?
   A. Community cloud
   B. Retail cloud
   C. Private cloud
   D. Public cloud

   ☑ **A.** Community clouds are used by organizations with the same type of computing needs.
   ☒ **B** is incorrect because there is no such thing as a retail cloud. **C** and **D** are incorrect because private clouds serve a single organization, while *public cloud* is a much too generic term; community cloud is the best answer.

Positive Indicators for Cloud Readiness

8. For which businesses would cloud computing be best suited? (Choose two.)
   A. Waterfront marketplace that thrives during the summer tourist season
   B. Rural medical practice with four employees
   C. Law enforcement agency
   D. A new company start-up that manufactures watercraft

☑   **A and D.** A waterfront marketplace that thrives seasonally means more computing resources are needed during certain times of the year; cloud computing provides elasticity, which means adding or removing computing services and user accounts as needed. New companies present a financial risk and may not have the desire to invest capital in computing resources on-site, so cloud computing offers an affordable solution without an expensive long-term commitment.
☒   **B and C** are incorrect. These choices are not great cloud computing candidates since they deal with very sensitive data that is protected by legislation.

Negative Indicators for Cloud Readiness

9. Which of the following are valid reasons for not adopting a cloud solution? (Choose two.)
    A. Local hardware is being fully utilized for unchanging IT workloads.
    B. The number of employees rarely changes.
    C. The number of employees changes often.
    D. A business experiences unpredictable project spikes throughout the year

☑   **A and B.** If local hardware is being fully and efficiently utilized for unchanging IT workloads, there is no benefit to using a cloud solution. Also, if the number of employees rarely changes, the business will not benefit from elasticity.
☒   **C and D** are incorrect because they are valid reasons for adopting a cloud solution.

Cloud Service Categories

10. As a developer for a software company, you have decided to build and test your web applications in a cloud environment. Which type of cloud service best meets your needs?
    A. PaaS
    B. SaaS
    C. IaaS
    D. XaaS

☑   **A.** Platform as a Service (PaaS) offers developers an inexpensive method by which they can develop and test their applications.
☒   **B** is incorrect because Software as a Service (SaaS) delivers end-user software over the Internet. **C** is incorrect because Infrastructure as a Service (Iaas) allows administrators to use cloud servers, storage, backup, networking, and so on. **D** does not apply since Anything as a Service (XaaS) is a generic term and PaaS is specific to the stated need.

2

Business Perspectives

Computing technology has touched every type of business, so it has become important to determine whether it enhances business offerings and productivity, as shown in Figure 2-1. Businesses (and individuals) are always looking at doing more with less, and cloud computing fits that mold.

Similarities and Differences Between Cloud Computing and Outsourcing

Cloud computing is about IT capabilities that are "rented" instead of "owned." These IT capabilities are delivered from a third-party service provider over a network, as shown in Figure 2-2. The consumer of cloud services uses the provider's hardware and software, which is located at the provider's facilities. The provider owns and maintains the hardware and software. The consumer and provider may be linked via the public Internet or a proprietary connection. Cloud computing does not mandate a specific technical implementation. It is about the use of technology,

FIGURE 2-1

Cloud computing new business promises

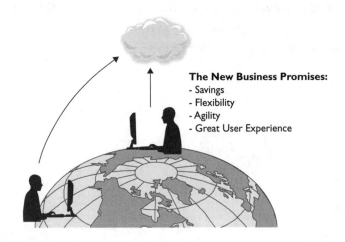

The New Business Promises:
- Savings
- Flexibility
- Agility
- Great User Experience

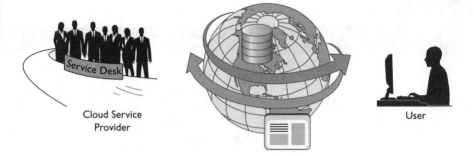

FIGURE 2-2

Cloud computing is about IT capabilities delivered as a service over a network.

Cloud Service Provider

User

not the configuration of technology. As such, it is a business model and not a specific technology.

From a business perspective, cloud computing is a form of outsourcing. Outsourcing is contracting a service of outside suppliers instead of providing those services via the company's own staff and assets.

Where cloud computing is specific to IT, outsourcing is not. With outsourcing, companies use outside professionals to complete specific activities. For example, businesses and individuals can hire a professional to prepare tax returns. The tax return is completed on your behalf, but you pay the outside entity to complete the work.

Recall that cloud computing elasticity allows for rapid provisioning of computing resources, so companies can quickly add or remove services. Outsourcing normally involves a long-term contract whose changes require renegotiation.

exam

ⓦatch *Any exam questions testing your knowledge of cloud computing versus outsourcing will probably be based on the fact that outsourcing requires more time to make contractual changes than a cloud service contract.*

Public cloud offerings are usually one-size-fits-all type of solutions, with some configuration options. Outsourcing tasks such as computing needs allows more granular computing offerings. For example, a business might outsource its help-desk needs for a specific line of business software, and the help-desk personnel would have expertise in this specific software. Table 2-1 compares cloud computing with outsourcing.

TABLE 2-1	Comparing Cloud Computing and Outsourcing	
	Cloud Computing	**Outsourcing**
Financial Commitment	Short term, can be changed in days or weeks	Long term, multiple years
Hardware and Software Assets	Limited options for client	Tailor-made for client
Scalability of Capacity	Practically instantaneous	Involves renegotiation or lead-time
	Access through web portal	Involves renegotiation

Reasons for Outsourcing

Outsourcing computing infrastructure needs has its advantages. Some of the reasons that drive this outsourcing are as follows:

- Cloud providers might have a lower cost per server because of their economies of scale.
- Managing an email system might not be considered a core competence, and an external provider that focuses on this may achieve a higher availability.
- Server procurement and provisioning consumes time and thus delays the time to market for important products.
- External service providers may provide access to innovative software solutions or platforms.
- Not owning a large data center full of servers reduces capital expenditure considerably.

Cloud Computing and Outsourcing Common Traits

Because cloud computing and outsourcing are similar, they share some common traits. The following conveys three business reasons you should consider when adopting either one:

- **Lack of internal skill set**   It is often wiser and cheaper over time to leave specialized skills to certified professionals.

- **Provider-owned assets**   You pay only for the computing resources you use instead of paying the full price for servers, storage, and computing power. Instead of spending capital on infrastructure, you can focus it on moving the business forward.
- **Vendor lock-in potential**   Once a contract with the supplier is in place, it becomes difficult to switch providers.

CERTIFICATION OBJECTIVE 2.02

Characteristics of Clouds and Cloud Services from a Business Perspective

Cloud computing is a business model, so using cloud services will offer great advantages. When a business adopts cloud computing, the impact resonates throughout the entire organization. Users will notice an improved experience and will also enjoy the reduced cost of usage.

Scalability

In a typical organization, IT represents a large and fairly inflexible investment. Without cloud computing, upgrading IT capacity can take as long as weeks or months, and downsizing is quite difficult. In addition, the development and rollout of new applications can also take months. Buying and deploying servers, installing software on them, configuring them, and getting ready for production can take a good deal of time and money.

on the **job**   *In the cloud, adding mailboxes, new servers, additional storage, and so on, is done via cloud provider web pages.*

Capacity Planning

In the cloud, provisioning additional computing resources is quick and easy; plus, you pay only for the resources you use. Figure 2-3 shows the traditional IT performance and cost problems that are minimized with proper capacity planning.

- **IaaS**   Computing resources, such as CPU and storage, can be added (*provisioned*) and released rapidly.

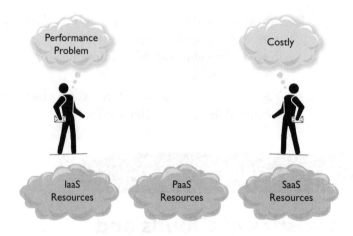

- **PaaS**   Application libraries are easily reused, which speeds up application development.
- **SaaS**   Users can be added and removed on short notice with few penalties.

Security

There are risks in every business, and every technology has its risks. The risks are often outweighed by the potential benefits of using this technology. Public cloud providers have the resources and expertise to provide a secure and isolated data environment between cloud customers. Combined with periodic independent third-party audits, it is reasonable to state that public cloud providers offer better security than most private organizations could provide by themselves.

Confidentiality

Confidentiality means that only authorized parties can view particular data. In IT, this is supported by encryption. Data is encrypted, or scrambled, so that only the parties in possession of the proper decryption key can access it. Industry or government regulations might not allow data to be stored in the cloud, even if it is encrypted.

Encryption applies to data being transmitted over a network as well as to stored data.

- **Network encryption**   The use of cloud services over the Internet means user-entered data, as well as user credentials to log on to cloud services, is being transmitted over the Internet. Most cloud services are delivered using Hypertext Transfer Protocol Secure (HTTPS). This is the encryption mechanism used for widely trusted secured web sites and is firewall-friendly, meaning most firewalls will allow this type of network traffic to pass through.

- ■ **Stored data** When files of any type are stored on some type of storage medium, encryption can be used to further secure the data. Data stored in the cloud can be encrypted with a customer-specific encryption key known only to the customer and not the cloud provider.

Some cloud providers have their own method of encrypting files stored in the cloud while other providers do not. For those providers that do not offer file encryption, cloud customers can use any encryption tool prior to uploading files to the cloud.

Integrity

Integrity ensures data has not been tampered with. Storing data in the cloud means there are potentially more people who could tamper with your data. However, cloud providers must pass vigorous third-party security audits on a recurring basis, so technically their data storage security and logging is probably far superior to the equivalent private business offering.

Availability

Business data must be readily available. Most cloud providers can replicate customer configurations and data between data centers. Your Internet service provider (ISP) normally controls your connection to cloud services, but without a reliable Internet connection, your data is inaccessible. Some cloud providers in some regions also control Internet connectivity to their services.

Cloud providers might offer load balancing, which is a way to distribute heavy network traffic destined to a specific service among multiple servers. The absence of redundant Internet connections leaves a single point of failure between employees and the computing services and data necessary for them to do their jobs.

Data confidentiality refers to encryption that allows access only to authorized users in possession of a decryption key. Data integrity ensures that data has not been tampered with.

How the Characteristics of Cloud Computing Enhance Business Value

Computer technicians eagerly sing the praises of cloud computing from a technical perspective, but where is the real value that solves business problems? Saving money and having an edge over competitors offers real value to any business. Keep reading to learn more about this.

Hardware Independence and Variable Costs

Cloud providers can deliver lower cost because they enjoy economies of scale. Clients don't have to purchase large amounts of hardware; instead, they are able to invest in cost-saving operational procedures, which are easy to justify.

In a typical organization, a large proportion of the effort is dedicated to maintaining the status quo in the face of updates, upgrades, and fixes. Operating systems need regular updates and patches in order to stay current and to fix emerging security problems. Log files and disk space need monitoring while application-software installations need updates, service packs, hotfixes, and so on. As demands on the systems change, continuous fine-tuning is necessary for the applications to continue working.

Cloud computing can considerably reduce the scope of work that has to be performed and, consequently, the amount of work. For example, most system-management tasks will be performed by the cloud service provider. This means businesses can enjoy smaller operating expenses (OPEX) over time instead of large initial capital expenditures (CAPEX), as depicted in Figure 2-4. On the other hand, it is not realistic to think that the entire IT budget will go away. Remember that users of cloud services still require a device with a web browser to connect to those cloud services, whether they use a smartphone, tablet, laptop, or desktop computer. Somebody has to pay for and maintain these devices.

e x a m

ⓦ a t c h   *Remember that cloud computing removes the need for large capital expenditures related to computing* *technology for the cloud customer. Instead, recurring subscription and usage fees become operating expenses.*

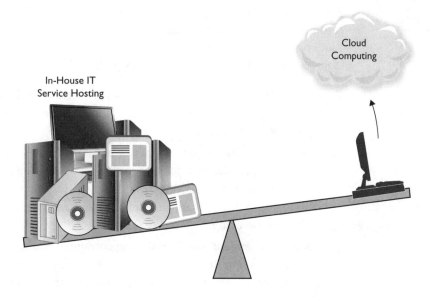

FIGURE 2-4

IT involves substantial capital expense.

In-House IT Service Hosting

Cloud Computing

Time to Market

For businesses, the ability to scale capacity up and down quickly is important. The deployment of servers might take too long for an organization to benefit from an emerging business opportunity. Agility is important. If you can move faster than your competitors, you can exploit transient market opportunities before they do. Agility means a shorter time to market, rapid innovation, increased market share, faster revenue growth, and superior customer loyalty. The key factor for agility is the time it takes to provision new hardware and software. Shorter lead times on IT investments increase the chance that an investment will become profitable before it becomes obsolete.

Distribution over the Internet

Public cloud services are available from any device anytime from anywhere in the world where you have an Internet connection. Instead of having to be in a physical office to access services and data, workers can be anywhere. Virtual private networks (VPNs) have facilitated this for many years, but VPNs normally require a hardware investment and IT expertise for configuration and maintenance.

Data collaboration is easily achieved since data is stored in the cloud. Cloud storage solutions offer document management, change tracking, revision history, and so on. This is far superior to emailing files to colleagues and requesting changes.

Business value can be something positive that has been added, but it can also be something negative that is reduced. Decision makers are always concerned with the cost and ongoing maintenance of business assets.

Companies might adopt a cloud computing model for the following reasons:

- Cloud providers have lower cost per server because of their economies of scale. Virtualization allows multiple cloud customers to share server hardware by way of virtual machines.

- Managing an email system might not be considered a core competence, and an external provider that focuses on that may achieve a higher availability. Nobody is good at everything. For example, a graphic sign design company does not specialize in managing email systems, and therefore hiring IT staff for this purpose might not make sense.

- Server procurement and provisioning consumes time and thus delays the time to market for important products. The cloud allows rapid provisioning; a newly needed server can come into existence in minutes. Without the cloud, it might take days or weeks to determine the hardware you need, wait for your order to ship, set up the equipment, install the required software and patches, and so on.

- External service providers may provide access to innovative software solutions or platforms. You might have access to solutions that otherwise would not be available within the organization.

- Not owning a large data center full of servers reduces capital expenditure considerably. A typical server room might represent thousands of dollars in capital expenditures; a data center could represent millions of dollars. Cloud providers already have this infrastructure; you just pay for what you use.

CERTIFICATION SUMMARY

This chapter took a look at cloud computing from a business perspective. Cloud IT services are rented as needed and, as such, can be quickly scaled to meet business needs. Outsourcing means enlisting professionals outside of the organization to complete specific tasks. Cloud computing is a form of outsourcing specific to IT.

Because of economies of scale, cloud providers are able to offer reasonable rates for the use of their services. This means instead of an organization tying up cash (capital expenses, or CAPEX) to invest in computing hardware, licensing, and maintenance, the cloud provider takes care of this. As a result, payment for cloud services becomes an operating expense (OPEX) to the cloud customer. Additionally, this frees up the organization to focus on their specific business and not on IT.

Cloud services across all types of providers share similar characteristics such as the rapid provisioning and deprovisioning, or *elasticity*, of IT services and on-demand access from any device. Public cloud providers have the resources and expertise, and they must pass periodic third-party audits, thus making their security practices second to none. Confidentiality ensures only authorized persons see appropriate data. Integrity ensures data has not been tampered with.

There must be a return in business value in order for cloud computing to be useful. Cloud services must always be available; cloud providers will normally configure their environments for high availability, but the cloud customer should have redundant network connections to eliminate this single point of failure.

✓ TWO-MINUTE DRILL

Similarities and Differences Between Cloud Computing and Outsourcing

❏ Cloud services are reachable over a network using a web browser and use provider hardware and expertise for IT solutions.

❏ Outsourcing uses outside expertise, whether it is IT related or not, to complete a specific business task.

❏ Cloud solutions allow rapid elasticity, whereas outsourcing takes more time to make contractual changes.

❏ The outsourcing of IT tasks allows tailor-made customer solutions.

❏ Vendor-lock is possible for both cloud computing and outsourcing.

Characteristics of Clouds and Cloud Services from a Business Perspective

❏ Scaling cloud services to meet your business needs is done quickly via cloud provider web pages.

❏ The redundancy of Internet links ensures the likelihood of your data always being available.

❏ Cloud providers take care of redundant servers, load balancing, and data storage.

❏ Data confidentiality protects data from unauthorized users via encryption.

❏ Data integrity protects data from being tampered with.

How the Characteristics of Cloud Computing Enhance Business Value

❏ Cloud computing shifts capital expenses to operating expenses.

❏ Without cloud computing, a business must purchase, install, configure, and maintain server computer systems.

❏ Businesses can focus on the timely realization of opportunities before their competitors do since they are not focused on the IT infrastructure.

❏ Data collaboration is facilitated when data is stored in the cloud.

SELF TEST

The following questions will help you measure your understanding of the material presented in this chapter. Read all the choices carefully because there might be more than one correct answer.

Similarities and Differences Between Cloud Computing and Outsourcing

1. How are cloud computing and outsourcing similar?
   - A. Immediate scalability
   - B. Vendor lock-in
   - C. Long contract renegotiation
   - D. Tailor-made client solutions

2. Which of the following is a benefit of outsourcing?
   - A. Immediate scalability
   - B. Vendor lock-in
   - C. Long contract renegotiation
   - D. Tailor-made client solutions

3. True or false? Cloud computing is a form of outsourcing.
   - A. True
   - B. False

Characteristics of Clouds and Cloud Services from a Business Perspective

4. What cloud computing characteristic ensures services and data are always reachable?
   - A. Confidentiality
   - B. Integrity
   - C. Availability
   - D. Scalability

5. You must ensure that your business computing resources can quickly grow as business demands change. Which of the following allows this?
   - A. Confidentiality
   - B. Integrity
   - C. Availability
   - D. Scalability

6. _____ protects data contents, while _____ ensures that data has not been tampered with.
   A. Availability, scalability
   B. Integrity, confidentiality
   C. Scalability, availability
   D. Confidentiality, integrity

How the Characteristics of Cloud Computing Enhance Business Value

7. Which of the following are related to cloud computing costs? (Choose two.)
   A. Monthly subscription
   B. Server hardware costs
   C. Usage fees
   D. Software licensing costs

8. How does cloud computing help an organization as new opportunities arise? (Choose two.)
   A. Shifting operating expenses to capital expenses
   B. Speedy addition of computing resources
   C. Less cost for new server hardware
   D. Speedy removal of computing resources

9. _____ and _____ give cloud customers a competitive advantage.
   A. Integrity, confidentiality
   B. Availability, integrity
   C. Time to market, collaboration
   D. Collaboration, confidentiality

SELF TEST ANSWERS

Similarities and Differences Between Cloud Computing and Outsourcing

1. How are cloud computing and outsourcing similar?
   A. Immediate scalability
   B. Vendor lock-in
   C. Long contract renegotiation
   D. Tailor-made client solutions

   ☑ **B.** Both cloud computing and outsourcing have the possibility of vendor lock-in once a contract for services has been agreed upon.
   ☒ **A, C,** and **D** are incorrect. Immediate scalability is a cloud computing characteristic, whereas outsourcing is characterized by longer contract renegotiations and custom client solutions.

2. Which of the following is a benefit of outsourcing?
   A. Immediate scalability
   B. Vendor lock-in
   C. Long contract renegotiation
   D. Tailor-made client solutions

   ☑ **D.** Public cloud solutions, specifically, SaaS, are often generalized IT software solutions. Outsourcing provides specific client solutions.
   ☒ **A, B,** and **C** are incorrect. Immediate scalability is a cloud computing characteristic. Vendor lock-in is not a positive potential and as such is not a benefit of outsourcing. Renegotiating contracts takes longer with outsourcing; cloud services allow rapid elasticity.

3. True or false? Cloud computing is a form of outsourcing.
   A. True
   B. False

   ☑ **A.** From a business perspective, cloud computing is a form of outsourcing.
   ☒ **B** is incorrect because cloud computing is a form of outsourcing.

Characteristics of Clouds and Cloud Services from a Business Perspective

4. What cloud computing characteristic ensures services and data are always reachable?
    A. Confidentiality
    B. Integrity
    C. Availability
    D. Scalability

    ☑   **C.** Availability ensures that something is reachable at any time.
    ☒   **A, B,** and **D** are incorrect. Confidentiality protects data from unauthorized users, while integrity ensures data has not been tampered with. Scalability refers to growing or shrinking capacity.

5. You must ensure that your business computing resources can quickly grow as business demands change. Which of the following allows this?
    A. Confidentiality
    B. Integrity
    C. Availability
    D. Scalability

    ☑   **D.** Scalability allows adding or removing computing resources in a cloud environment.
    ☒   **A, B,** and **C** are incorrect. Confidentiality and integrity are related to data security. Availability ensures data and services are always reachable.

6. _____ protects data contents, while _____ ensures that data has not been tampered with.
    A. Availability, scalability
    B. Integrity, confidentiality
    C. Scalability, availability
    D. Confidentiality, integrity

    ☑   **D.** Confidentiality protects data contents, while integrity ensures that data has not been tampered with.
    ☒   **A, B,** and **C** are incorrect. Availability and scalability do not have anything to do with protecting data. **B** is incorrect because the terms are in the wrong order.

How the Characteristics of Cloud Computing Enhance Business Value

7. Which of the following are related to cloud computing costs? (Choose two.)
- A. Monthly subscription
- B. Server hardware costs
- C. Usage fees
- D. Software licensing costs

☑ **A** and **C.** Cloud providers charge customers a monthly subscription fee as well as resource usage fees. Resources might be cloud servers, CPU usage, storage space, and so on.
☒ **B** and **D** are incorrect. They are costs associated with the on-premises acquisition of hardware and software.

8. How does cloud computing help an organization as new opportunities arise? (Choose two.)
- A. Shifting operating expenses to capital expenses
- B. Speedy addition of computing resources
- C. Less cost for new server hardware
- D. Speedy removal of computing resources

☑ **B** and **D.** With many businesses, time to market is critical. The ability to quickly add and remove computing resources cheaply allows acting upon business opportunities quickly.
☒ **A** and **C** are incorrect. Cloud computing shifts capital expenses to operating expenses, not the other way around. Cheaper server hardware is great, but as a cloud customer, acquiring server hardware is kept at a minimum, if it is done at all.

9. _____ and _____ give cloud customers a competitive advantage.
- A. Integrity, confidentiality
- B. Availability, integrity
- C. Time to market, collaboration
- D. Collaboration, confidentiality

☑ **C.** Businesses have competitors. Getting products and services to the market before competitors is an advantage. Convenient collaboration between employees is critical to the success of any organization; everybody has their specific strengths. Data is made available from anywhere using any device with cloud storage.
☒ **A, B,** and **D** are incorrect. They are not specific advantages related to the cloud.

3
Technical Perspectives

T he cloud landscape is an abundantly developing field with lots of new approaches that are competing and oftentimes incompatible. At the same time, vendors, products, and solutions come and go. Properly navigating this developing landscape can make the difference between successful and failed cloud deployments.

CERTIFICATION OBJECTIVE 3.01

Differences Between Public and Private Clouds

The main difference between private and public clouds is that private clouds are provisioned for exclusive use by a single organization. Public clouds offer IT services to anybody with an Internet connection.

Private Clouds

Private clouds give an organization control over their own data security and resource access. Private clouds can be owned, managed, and operated by an organization, a third party, or a combination of both. This means a private cloud may exist on or off the premises or both.

Departments or business units within an organization are treated as cloud resource consumers, and they benefit from elastic rapid provisioning and scalability of compute resources. As a result, an organization realizes a more efficient and productive use of its investment in IT.

Figure 3-1 shows a private network of cloud computing resources available only to business units within an organization. Technically, the computing resources do not have to be hosted on the premises; they just have to be made available for the exclusive use of the organization on a private network.

Aside from configuring the private cloud infrastructure, or *fabric*, resource use must be monitored continuously to ensure proper resource distribution and control. You can think of a cloud fabric as the collective networking, storage, and processing capabilities available to cloud consumers.

For example, you might monitor virtual server usage for chargeback to a specific business unit. Products such as VMware's vCenter Chargeback and Microsoft's

FIGURE 3-1

Example of a
private cloud
infrastructure

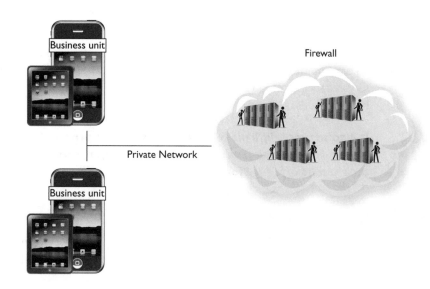

System Center 2012 SP1 Service Manager allow metering of cloud resources based
on consumption. These tools can be used for both public and private clouds.

e x a m

ⓦ**a t c h**   *The operative phrase to*   *Questions using this phrase are most likely*
watch for on the exam is "exclusive use."   *referring to a private cloud solution.*

Public Clouds

Where private clouds are for exclusive use by a single business, public clouds offer
computing services to anybody who has an Internet connection. For example, Internet
users might subscribe to the Dropbox file-hosting service for cloud file storage.

Public clouds do not give consumers control of computing resources. Private
clouds are characterized by exclusive use of resources by a single organization on a
private network; public clouds do not offer a private network for each customer.

Hybrid Clouds

Hybrid clouds are a combination of private and public clouds. For example, consider an organization using its local user accounts to authenticate to multiple public cloud services such as cloud email and cloud storage. The key phrase to remember about hybrid clouds is "multiple providers."

on the job   *It is sometimes difficult to distinguish between private, public, and hybrid clouds. For example, some cloud providers offer private hosted versions of their public offerings for exclusive use by a single organization.*

Cloud Computing Service Models

Chapter 1 discussed the three main cloud computing service models, as shown in Figure 3-2. We will explore some further considerations regarding each of these three models.

FIGURE 3-2

SaaS, PaaS, and IaaS

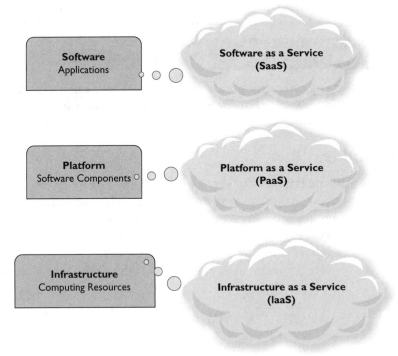

Software as a Service (SaaS)

The attraction of Software as a Service is that using it in its simplest form requires only a web browser, a URL, an Internet connection, and credentials such as a username and password. Ideally, this simplicity offers a lot more device and location independence than applications that are developed and deployed to a local office environment.

In reality, some limitations apply. For example, not every application is conveniently accessed on mobile devices, and some applications are actually very demanding in the number of browsers they need to work well. This is depicted in Figure 3-3.

SaaS applications may also need connections to other enterprise applications. For example, an HR application would need personnel records, while a sales application might need to share its order information with a financial application. These connections might be made in one or more of the following ways:

- **Uploading or downloading data sets**   You might migrate local data to the cloud (upload) so that your cloud SaaS app can use it. For disconnected users (a rarity these days in most parts of the world), data can be downloaded to their devices so it is available to them when they are offline.

- **Web services**   Cloud apps connect to each other using web standards to exchange data, often in XML format. eXtensible Markup Language (XML) uses data descriptor tags to present data in a simple fashion and is used extensively to share data between dissimilar systems.

A SaaS application is by definition multitenant. SaaS apps are built with multiple users in mind, and they are optimized for remote use.

FIGURE 3-3

Software as a Service

www.url.com
Name
****

Independence of Device and Location

Not Compatible with All Browsers

Customization of the application either is a client-configurable option or is done through add-ons, plug-ins, or web services. None of these involves any change in the core application software. As for security, SaaS providers must ensure that one customer cannot access information from another customer. Note that there is already an obligation to make sure two users of the same customer can see each other's information only if authorized properly.

Platform as a Service (PaaS)

PaaS is of interest to software developers; it enables the creation of a rich universe of application components and services that can be used by other applications, all delivered over a network. Table 3-1 lists scopes of PaaS along with examples.

Traditionally, creating, testing, and maintaining software applications was costly and complex. This is because investments in hardware, software, licensing, and networking infrastructure were required. To make matters worse, after a specific application development project, the investment in computing resources might not be used to its full capacity, therefore representing waste.

Now, how does PaaS technically work? Most of these platforms are accessed through web services. A web service is an application programming interface (API) that looks like a web server and can be accessed through URLs. These URLs encode the operations to be performed. The parameters for these calls are then also part of the URL, or they are transmitted using the HTTP POST operation. Results are transmitted back as an XML or JSON document, or possibly even plain, unformatted text. Although PaaS applications are intended to be used by other applications anywhere on the Internet, they can also be accessed using an ordinary browser.

TABLE 3-1   PaaS Scopes and Examples

Scope	Example
Narrow	These types include specific data sets and databases and handle very specific functions. Examples include the Google Maps API or a postal code lookup service.
Dedicated	These types are focused on a specific domain but allow some programming. Force.com, which accompanies Salesforce.com, can be used by a web site to enter new customers into a Salesforce database.
General	These provide a general-purpose programming platform with generic functions such as database and messaging functions. Examples include Microsoft Azure, Google AppEngine, Heroku, Engine Yard, and the open source CloudFoundry.

For example, consider the following URL to a web service:

http://ws.geonames.org/postalCodeSearch?postalcode=90210&country=us

Here we are accessing a web service called *postalCodeSearch* on a web server called *ws.geonames.org* and providing the postal code *90210* and the country *us* as parameters. The web service results in a web page telling us that 90210 is the postal code for Beverly Hills, California, and it also provides the longitude and latitude coordinates.

PaaS is also the way rich Internet applications (RIAs) are made. An RIA is a web application with many of the characteristics of desktop applications. It is typically delivered by way of a site-specific browser, a browser plug-in, independent sandboxes, or virtual machines. The web page that is initially loaded in the browser displays some text and images, while in the background it executes JavaScript that asynchronously makes additional calls to web services using XML as the data format for queries and responses. These additional calls bring in more text and graphics.

Together, these techniques are called Ajax (for asynchronous JavaScript and XML). For example, Ajax is used in http://maps.google.com. Each time you zoom or pan to a different location, the new map parts are brought in asynchronously. In addition, a lot of the Twitter user interfaces are built this way.

e x a m

Ⓦ **a t c h**   One drawback of PaaS is the potential for vendor lock-in. A PaaS provider might provide a specific interface   and tools to create web services that are incompatible with other PaaS providers.

Infrastructure as a Service (IaaS)

Of all cloud services, Infrastructure as a Service most resembles the components that can be found in a modern data center, even though IaaS could actually be in different locations. IasS includes storage, firewalls, load balancers, physical or virtual servers, and networks, to name a few. The traditional server environment consists of a number of layers of technology. Virtualization adds a new layer that isolates the software components of the stack from the hardware layers.

Server Virtualization   Server virtualization allows the sharing of underlying hardware. Multiple virtual machines (VMs) can run concurrently and independently on the same physical hardware. The VMs can be powered on, powered off, and rebooted independently of each other. You can install a different operating system and applications into each separate VM to create virtual, or "cloud" servers. Figure 3-4 shows four virtual machines running different operating systems: Windows Server 2003, Windows Server 2008, Red Hat Enterprise Linux, and OpenSolaris.

Creating a virtual server in the cloud involves the following steps:

1. Log in to the cloud provider web portal using a management account.
2. Select a virtual machine image or template that defines the operating system and optionally software applications.
3. Select security credentials for logging into the server that will be created.
4. Select firewall settings for the virtual server.
5. Select an instance type to indicate which resources (storage, processor speed, amount of RAM) will be available to the virtual server.

After a few minutes, your server is ready to be accessed over the Internet if using a public cloud provider. Private clouds make the virtual server accessible over a private network. Either way, this is much quicker and does not require a capital expenditure,

FIGURE 3-4

Server virtualization allows multiple VMs to share the same hardware.

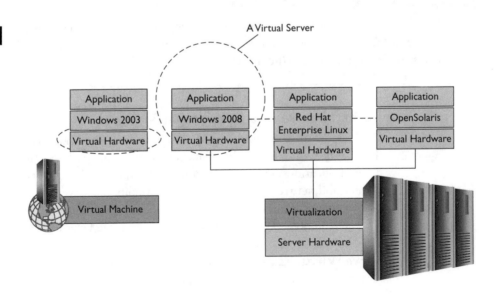

Creating a
Windows Server
2012 virtual
server

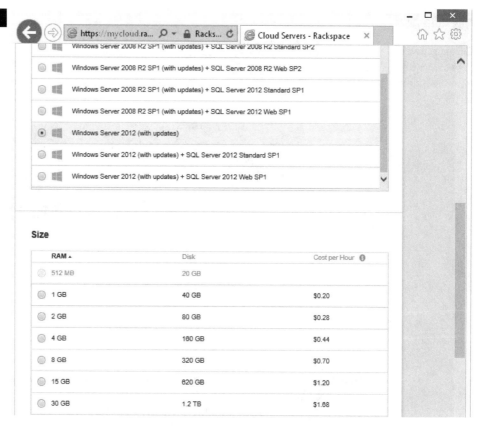

as buying a physical server would. Figure 3-5 shows the Rackspace.com web page for creating a Windows Server 2012 virtual server.

Content Distribution Network   Content distribution networks (CDNs) are a way to improve the performance and speed of web-based services by relocating content. A typical web site is composed of an HTML file containing references to the content of the site, for example, a number of pictures (see Figure 3-6). Through a CDN service, these pictures will be served from cloud data centers much closer to the web browsers.

The domain name of the CDN—static.mycdn.com in Figure 3-6—is mapped to a different edge server, depending on the location of the web browser. The CDN typically does this through the Domain Name System (DNS).

FIGURE 3-6

Clients get web
page content
from the nearest
server.

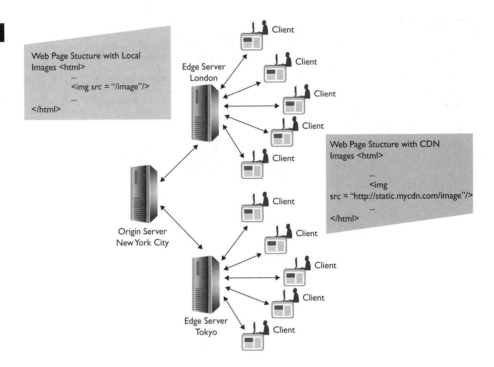

Cloud-Based Storage   Hundreds of web sites exist that give users storage on demand. Examples include Dropbox, Box.net, and Google Docs. They differ in functionality, but the commonality is that they are accessed through a web site. In some ways, they resemble SaaS applications.

Cloud-based storage can also be accessed via a web service (PaaS). The storage itself is considered infrastructure and is therefore IaaS. Some cloud providers allow you to deploy storage separately from virtual servers so that the storage is treated similarly to a storage area network (SAN), where the storage is not owned by a specific single server.

Virtual Appliances   A virtual appliance is a virtual server packaged with specific software for a specific use. For example, a cloud provider might provide a deployable web server appliance as well as a database server appliance. They can be used in either a public or private cloud environment and facilitate deployment for nontechnical users.

Cloud Management and Auditing Services   A cloud consumer is likely to have a relationship with multiple cloud providers, which provide a complex and rapidly changing set of services. Independent services exist that audit and manage this. Examples include monitoring performance and uptime of cloud services, tracking cloud spending, tracking configuration changes, validating security and compliance objectives, and orchestrating the deployment of cloud components.

CERTIFICATION OBJECTIVE 3.02

Techniques and Methods for Cloud Computing Deployment

Cloud deployments have many technical similarities to other IT-system deployments, but they differ in how resources are provisioned (see "Cloud Computing Characteristics" in Chapter 1). Networking, automation, self-service, federation, and the increased importance of standards are paramount to a successful cloud deployment.

Networking

All forms of cloud computing depend on networking. The following are the key considerations of network design as they relate to cloud computing:

- **Locations**   An organization's private network consists of switches and routers interconnecting network devices behind corporate firewalls. With cloud computing, IT services are delivered to clients anywhere using any type of device.
- **Bandwidth**   This defines how quickly data can be moved over a wired or wireless connection. Local area networks (LANs) are contained in a single location, such as an office building or university campus and therefore enjoy high bandwidth. Because cloud computing clients can be anywhere (especially public cloud clients), bandwidth considerations are paramount.
- **Latency tolerance**   Cloud computing serves clients at spread-out locations, and you should expect an increase in transmission delays. Not all applications tolerate these delays.

- **Firewalls and access control** This can be configured in the cloud, locally on premises, or both. For example, using IaaS cloud servers and networks implies the use of a private cloud network. Some providers allow you to use your existing IP address structure in the cloud. This private cloud network might have configurable firewall options. Cloud servers (virtual servers) always have their own firewall settings.

- **Resilience and redundancy** Virtual servers, clustering, load balancing, cloud storage, backup, data replication—these all ensure that computing services are highly available and that there are multiple copies of the data they produce.

Automation and Self-Service

Traditionally, IT systems are built with engineering diagrams and work orders, which are then executed by IT operations, and this can take weeks. Cloud-computing service models allow that to be done through self-service web sites and web services, which can take merely minutes.

Automation is the key to reducing operational expenses. How automation is implemented depends on the existing capabilities of the organization. The desirable end state is where business requirements are input to a service orchestration tool or function that automatically configures entire application server stacks and automatically provisions and deprovisions servers, as load varies. According to the National Institute of Standards and Technology (NIST), "Service Orchestration refers to the composition of system components to support the Cloud Providers' activities in arrangement, coordination and management of computing resources in order to provide cloud services to Cloud Consumers." Microsoft Azure (IaaS and PaaS) is a good example of cloud automation; on a single day, thousands of private cloud networks might be created to accommodate cloud customer demand. Having this done manually by humans would take much longer and would be prone to error.

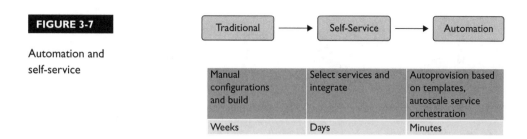

FIGURE 3-7

Automation and
self-service

Public cloud self-service portals will charge fees as computing resources are provisioned and used. Private cloud self-service portals will often use departmental chargeback, or some kind of quota system such that once the configured quota points are exhausted, no further resources can be provisioned. Figure 3-7 summarizes the time used when provisioning compute resources.

Federation

Access to information systems is granted through digital identities that might come in the form of a username and password or *Public Key Infrastructure* (PKI) certificates. When multiple services from different providers are used, it becomes desirable to separate identity management from applications. This is done through one or more *identity providers*. The use of one or more identity providers across multiple applications is called *identity federation*, and it reduces the number of accounts and passwords that users have to remember, and it reduces identity management tasks.

Identity providers are known as *issuing parties* because they issue credentials. The SaaS providers then act as a relying party, because it relies on the issuing party. The relying parties (application or service providers) decide about the access rights (authorization) themselves. Users can use their digital identities at multiple SaaS providers; this is also known as *single sign-on* (SSO). Social networks such as Twitter and Facebook have proven to be convenient identity providers on the Internet, as shown in Figure 3-8. Some SaaS providers even facilitate the use of company-identity credentials, such as those residing in Microsoft's Active Directory. This would allow users to authenticate with their corporate credentials and gain access to cloud services without a separate username and password.

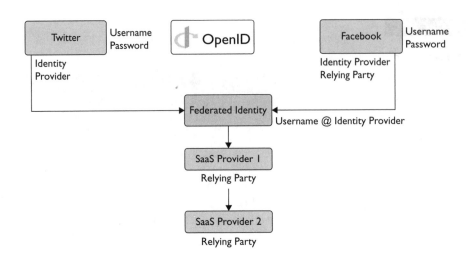

FIGURE 3-8

Twitter and Facebook acting as identity providers for relying party applications

Standardization

Organizations adopting the cloud should select providers that perform the right amount of standardization on the types of services that are used. Properly used, standardization improves interconnection and interoperability between services. Standardization should be part of a cloud customer's exit strategy; standardized service configurations might be exportable from one provider and importable to another. However, when overdone, standardization restricts innovation.

Vendor lock-in occurs when cloud provider solutions use proprietary settings and tools instead of widely accepted standards. Cloud customers should look at standardization in their cloud provider offerings. An example might be a PaaS provider allowing developers to build web services that use XML to transmit information and allowing developers to export the web service definition to a text file; these are standards that allow web services to interact with dissimilar systems and also to be imported into other environments. Here are some examples of relevant standards you should look for:

- **Data formats**   These include eXtensible Markup Language (XML) and JavaScript Object Notation (JSON).
- **Data storage**   Being able to move data from cloud to cloud reduces lock-in to a storage provider. This might include the option to export cloud data to a standard file format that can be imported to a different cloud storage provider.

- ■ **Standard virtual machine images** This offers the ability to move a virtual machine from one cloud to another.
- ■ **Standard application programming interface (API)** This allows for provisioning web services in order to prevent vendor lock-in.
- ■ **Identity information standards** These include Open Authorization (OAuth), OpenID, and Security Assertion Markup Language (SAML).

CERTIFICATION OBJECTIVE 3.03

Cloud Computing Risks and Challenges

Cloud technology eliminates some existing risks, such as lack of capacity or slow deployment, but introduces new risks. The risks originate from different technical characteristics in a networked environment, from the potential openness of systems, and from the fact that resources are shared.

Application Performance

In a cloud environment, the most likely culprit that will affect application performance is the network link separating cloud clients and cloud servers. The performance and speed of network links are described by terms such as *bandwidth* and *latency*.

Bandwidth and Latency

As mentioned earlier in this chapter, *bandwidth* defines how quickly data can be moved over a wired or wireless connection. The amount of time it takes for data to travel from one end of a network link to the other is called *transmission latency*. Cloud providers in some regions offer bundled network connectivity with a guaranteed speed (part of the SLA), but normally your Internet service provider controls your network speed, and this is often separate from your cloud provider agreement.

Remember, cloud services are not hosted locally; they are delivered over a network. The network connection is your single point of failure. Figure 3-9 shows a geographically distributed collection of cities using cloud services. Network connectivity to cloud services should be fast and reliable; otherwise, the impact on productivity will be negative. You should consider multiple network paths to your cloud provider in case one fails or becomes too congested.

FIGURE 3-9

Network bandwidth vs. latency: what's the difference?

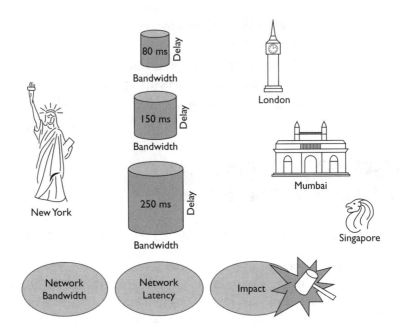

CPU

The central processing unit (CPU) is the core of any computing device; it is the brain that performs all calculations. Both physical and virtual servers might have a single-core processor (one CPU) or multiple-core processor. Depending on the application load, more cores might improve performance. Some applications require vast amounts of memory and little CPU processing power, and other applications might require the opposite or both. On the client side, cloud computing does not require significant CPU processing power since most SaaS cloud apps are provided in a web browser.

Storage Access Speed

Another challenge with cloud storage is that it is never as fast as local disks can be. This challenge is likely to grow worse over time since data volumes are growing faster than network bandwidth. This is relevant in normal operation, which includes cloud backups, and when performing imports and exports. For normal operation, the implication is that data storage must be physically close to any heavy processing that must be done with it. Moving either large data sets or complete virtual machines in and out of a particular cloud is not to be taken lightly.

Data Replication

When using cloud computing, applications are likely to be spread over multiple providers, whether for technical, business, or regulatory reasons. It then becomes a new challenge to keep the master data of these applications synchronized. Some examples of master data are customer account information, catalog data, and user identities. A number of approaches are possible for realizing the necessary data synchronization.

- Replicate a master copy of the data to all applications hosted by all providers. This requires careful attention to how often replication occurs.
- Synchronize all data changes in all directions when changes occur. This can be difficult to implement as it may require the use of additional tools.
- Rather than replicating data, data can be looked up in real time at a central source. The benefit is that the data is always up to date, but the drawback is network latency.

Data Integration

When using cloud services, it is possible for cloud software to communicate with on-premises software. Integrating data in real time in a hybrid cloud environment once again depends on the quality and speed of your network connection. Viewed from a different perspective, data integration involves importing data from your on-premises systems into the cloud so that cloud software can use that data. Either way, make sure you have a redundant and reliable network link.

Network Security

Security in cloud computing is not harder overall; it is just different. Perhaps the most fundamental difference is that there is no longer a simple network perimeter with all the organization's users and servers on one side and the Internet on the other side, as shown in Figure 3-10. Cloud clients could potentially be connecting from thousands of different networks that are not under central control. The result is that individual cloud components, such as cloud servers, must have individual firewalls.

FIGURE 3-10

Traditional
perimeter
network security
does not apply
like it used to.

CERTIFICATION OBJECTIVE 3.04

The Impact of Cloud Computing on Application Development and Architecture

Cloud computing, specifically PaaS, makes new building blocks available to application developers. This means rapid application development, testing, and deployment compared to traditional on-premises methods.

Development Process

Any software-development process requires translating functional and nonfunctional requirements into a working solution providing services to a user community. This does not change with cloud computing. What does change is the set of building blocks on which this is done.

Cloud computing provides a large ecosystem of prebuilt components that can be used. Performance and scalability requirements are more easily met, some traditional risks disappear, and new risks arise. The traditional waterfall model (design, build, order hardware, and install) changes. Instead, the cloudscape must be inventoried for existing services and components. This includes SaaS, PaaS, and IaaS services. Then, building the system often consists of configuring existing services.

Application Architecture

Application architecture describes how an application is subdivided into components, together with the relations that these components have, in addition to the relations that these applications have with other applications. Contemporary applications are built in layers: clients, presentation, business logic, and database. Application development with cloud computing can change all these layers.

- **Building blocks** The building blocks of the applications can exist in the cloud, outside the traditional perimeter of the organization. This is true for SaaS, where most of the application will be in the cloud. It is also true for PaaS, where application components simply exist as services in the cloud.
- **Target platform** Even when building blocks are developed, the target platform can be in the cloud. These IaaS components may deviate in a number of ways from their traditional data center equivalents, for example, in the models that are available to scale them.
- **Service-oriented architecture** In general, cloud computing encourages a service-oriented architecture, where information is shipped between applications and application components through the use of web services.

CERTIFICATION SUMMARY

Cloud solutions use technology to serve varying business needs. Private clouds run on computing infrastructure owned by an organization, and the private cloud services are for exclusive use by that organization. Cloud services can be metered for departmental chargeback.

Public clouds offer IT services to all organizations and Internet users, and these users normally have a monthly subscription fee (essentially, "pay as you go"). Hybrid cloud combine private and public clouds. For example, a company might use its private cloud during normal business activity and use public cloud services to handle additional business activity.

SaaS allows end users to access productivity software using a web browser, anytime, from a wide range of devices. PaaS allows software developers to quickly create and test applications or web services.

IaaS offers computing infrastructure resources such as virtual servers, cloud storage, cloud networks, and so on, to be rented as needed by cloud customers. Virtualization hides physical hardware from a running guest operating system so that multiple virtual machines can run concurrently on a single physical server. This is required for rapid provisioning and deprovisioning of cloud IaaS services, and it is much quicker than traditional server procurement.

Because cloud services are delivered over a network (such as the Internet), fast and redundant network connections should be considered; the network connection presents a single point of failure. Cloud providers ensure there is not a single point of failure with their configurations; service availability will be outlined in the SLA.

Self-service is a cloud characteristic that allows cloud subscribers to use a web portal to add or remove cloud service components, such as adding new email accounts for newly hired employees or adding a new virtual server to handle an increase in business volume.

Authorizing users to access cloud services is possible by creating user identities in the cloud, but most organizations already have user identities on their own authentication servers. Identity federation allows users authenticated within an organization to get authorized to cloud services, all without re-creating or replicating user accounts to the cloud.

Risks such as network latency, lack of cloud provider data standardization, or a cloud provider going out of business must be considered when evaluating cloud solutions.

Rapid application development and testing is possible with PaaS because of how quickly virtual machines can be provisioned and because of prebuilt application components. Efficiency is achieved when application development projects are completed and IT services infrastructure are deprovisioned.

TWO-MINUTE DRILL

Differences Between Public and Private Clouds

❑ Public clouds are available to all Internet users and charge their customers subscription and metered usage fees.

❑ Public clouds offer limited control of resources and security.

❑ Public clouds are considered more secure than private clouds.

❑ Private clouds are for the exclusive use of a single organization and imply the use of private networks.

❑ Private clouds might track and charge resource usage to departments within the organization.

❑ SaaS, PaaS, and IaaS offer varying types of computing services to public and private cloud users.

❑ SaaS offers applications to end users over the network.

❑ PaaS provides building blocks for application developers (APIs) that take the form of web services, often using standards such as XML and JSON.

❑ IaaS provides server virtualization, which allows multiple virtual machines to run a single piece of server hardware. Each virtual machine is completely independent of another.

❑ IaaS provides content distribution networks (CDNs), which use DNS to direct end users to the nearest web site content.

❑ Both public and private cloud resource usage must be managed, monitored, and metered for billing or chargeback.

Techniques and Methods for Cloud Computing Deployment

❑ Network bandwidth measures the speed at which data is sent over a connection.

❑ Latency measures network transmission delay.

❑ Cloud servers use host-based firewalls.

❑ Provisioning of cloud resources is expedited through the use of automation and self-service web portals.

❑ Federation allows SSO for applications that might be hosted across multiple cloud providers. The identity source can be an organization's local user accounts or cloud identities.

❑ Standardization allows cloud components to interoperate with other cloud components, even between different cloud providers.

Cloud Computing Risks and Challenges

❑ High bandwidth and low latency are desirable for optimal application performance.

❑ Cloud data access is also optimized with high-bandwidth, low-latency network connections.

❑ Virtual servers can be configured with one or more CPUs; some applications are processor intensive.

❑ An organization's data might need to be synchronized between different cloud applications or between a cloud application and a locally hosted application.

❑ Business data can be imported to the cloud for use by cloud software, or it can be exported from the cloud for use elsewhere.

❑ The network distribution of cloud clients means traditional firewall methods may not be enough; cloud providers have the resources to properly handle network security with host-based firewalls, private networks, third-party audits, and so on.

The Impact of Cloud Computing on Application Development and Architecture

❑ PaaS gives developers building blocks used to create custom cloud solutions.

❑ The cloud allows rapid provisioning of virtual machines and storage used to create, test, and deploy these custom cloud solutions that can be deprovisioned when not needed.

SELF TEST

The following questions will help you measure your understanding of the material presented in this chapter. Read all the choices carefully because there might be more than one correct answer.

Differences Between Public and Private Clouds

I. Which of the following statements are true? (Choose two.)
   A. Public clouds are for the exclusive use of a single organization.
   B. Private clouds are for the exclusive use of a single organization.
   C. Public clouds are offered over an intranet.
   D. Public clouds are offered over the Internet.

2. True or false? Virtual servers are used only in public clouds.
   A. True
   B. False

3. When creating cloud virtual servers, which of the following must be specified? (Choose two.)
   A. Username and password
   B. Server name
   C. IP address
   D. Operating system licensing

Techniques and Methods for Cloud Computing Deployment

4. You are linking your company's Microsoft Active Directory user accounts to your cloud provider for federated identity management. What type of configuration must you create within your company?
   A. Identity trust
   B. XML provider
   C. Relying party trust
   D. JSON provider

5. Your public cloud environment is configured such that additional cloud storage is allocated to a virtual server when the used disk space on that server reaches more than 80 percent of disk capacity. Which term best describes this configuration?
   A. Elasticity
   B. Automation
   C. Self-service
   D. Disk latency

Cloud Computing Risks and Challenges

6. Which of the following might factor into an exit strategy for a cloud customer?
   A. Vendor lock-in
   B. Self-service
   C. Standardization
   D. Automation

7. Which of the following is not considered a cloud computing risk?
   A. Loss of network connectivity
   B. Data stored in the cloud
   C. Network latency
   D. Host-based firewalls

The Impact of Cloud Computing on Application Development and Architecture

8. What is a benefit of PaaS?
   A. Rapid application development
   B. Replication
   C. High bandwidth
   D. Low latency

9. Developers build these components in the cloud.
   A. Federation identity providers
   B. Cloud load balancers
   C. SaaS user mailboxes
   D. Web services

SELF TEST ANSWERS

Differences Between Public and Private Clouds

1. Which of the following statements are true? (Choose two.)
   A. Public clouds are for the exclusive use of a single organization.
   B. Private clouds are for the exclusive use of a single organization.
   C. Public clouds are offered over an intranet.
   D. Public clouds are offered over the Internet.

   ☑ **B and D.** Private clouds are for the exclusive use of a single organization. Public cloud offerings are accessible over the Internet.
   ☒ **A and C.** Public clouds are not for the exclusive use of a single organization; anybody on the Internet can subscribe. Public clouds are offered over the Internet, not an intranet within an organization.

2. True or false? Virtual servers are used only in public clouds.
   A. True
   B. False

   ☑ **B.** Cloud computing uses virtualization, but virtualization does not need cloud computing.
   ☒ **A.** Virtual servers are usable not only in public clouds; they can be used anywhere.

3. When creating cloud virtual servers, which of the following must be specified? (Choose two,)
   A. Username and password
   B. Server name
   C. IP address
   D. Operating system licensing

   ☑ **A and B.** Each cloud virtual server requires that you specify security credentials for the server as well as a server name used in the cloud environment.
   ☒ **C and D** are incorrect because they are not required when creating a cloud virtual server.

Techniques and Methods for Cloud Computing Deployment

4. You are linking your company's Microsoft Active Directory user accounts to your cloud provider for federated identity management. What type of configuration must you create within your company?
   A. Identity trust
   B. XML provider
   C. Relying party trust
   D. JSON provider

   > ☑ **C.** Since your company is the identity provider, you must trust the relying party offering services, so you must configure a relying party trust.
   >
   > ☒ **A, B,** and **D** are incorrect. In the question, the cloud provider would configure an identity trust, not you. XML and JSON are not specifically related to configuring identity federation.

5. Your public cloud environment is configured such that additional cloud storage is allocated to a virtual server when the used disk space on that server reaches more than 80 percent of disk capacity. Which term best describes this configuration?
   A. Elasticity
   B. Automation
   C. Self-service
   D. Disk latency

   > ☑ **B.** If storage space is allocated automatically based on a configured threshold, it is automation.
   >
   > ☒ **A, C,** and **D** are incorrect. Elasticity is a close second here, but it does not imply the automatic provisioning of resources. Automation is a better answer. Self-service allows users to provision the computing resources they need using a web site, but it is not automatic. Disk latency refers to the amount of time taken to read data from a disk and is not related to automation.

Cloud Computing Risks and Challenges

6. Which of the following might factor into an exit strategy for a cloud customer?
   A. Vendor lock-in
   B. Self-service
   C. Standardization
   D. Automation

   ☑ **C.** Standardization allows cloud customers to move web services or data between cloud providers.
   ☒ **A, B,** and **D** are incorrect. Vendor lock-in works against a cloud customer's exit strategy since it implies methods and components specific to that cloud provider. Self-service and automation are related to the provisioning of cloud IT resources and have nothing to do with exit strategies.

7. Which of the following is not considered a cloud computing risk?
   A. Loss of network connectivity
   B. Data stored in the cloud
   C. Network latency
   D. Host-based firewalls

   ☑ **D.** Host-based firewalls are not a risk; they mitigate network attacks.
   ☒ **A, B,** and **C** are incorrect because they are all risks associated with cloud computing.

The Impact of Cloud Computing on Application Development and Architecture

8. What is a benefit of PaaS?
   A. Rapid application development
   B. Replication
   C. High bandwidth
   D. Low latency

   ☑ **A.** Rapid application development is possible with PaaS because servers, databases, and other components used by developers can be made available within minutes instead of requesting hardware and software from a local IT department.
   ☒ **B, C,** and **D** are incorrect because they are not related directly to PaaS.

9. Developers build these components in the cloud.
   A. Federation identity providers
   B. Cloud load balancers
   C. SaaS user mailboxes
   D. Web services

☑ **D.** Developers can build web services in the cloud. Web services are small web applications that run on web servers and are accessible through a URL that may include parameters needed by the web service.

☒ **A, B,** and **C** are incorrect because they are not components built in the cloud by developers; they are cloud components built by IT administrators.

4

Adopting Cloud Computing

Different organizations have different objectives for adopting the cloud. This includes making changes to the way people work, the types of skills needed in the organization, and the relationship of the organization and its users to its IT providers.

Typical Steps Leading to Successful Cloud Adoption

For an organization, cloud adoption can be a complex undertaking. As a result, no two companies will follow the same cloud adoption steps. For an individual user, a failed cloud adoption will have a less profound effect. The following are the typical cloud adoption steps, with each being detailed throughout this chapter:

- Choose a low-risk application for a cloud pilot.
- Consider which cloud service models best meet the business objectives (SaaS, IaaS, or PaaS).
- Consider cloud provider roles and capabilities.
- Examine your dependencies on cloud providers and perform a risk assessment.
- Determine possible changes to organizational roles and skills.

Before delving into what a successful cloud adoption consists of, we will dispel myths related to cloud computing.

Cloud Computing Myths

Over the years some misconceptions related to cloud computing have emerged. The most common fallacies are listed below:

- **"There is a single good level of cloud adoption."** This is a myth. There are various strategic options, such as don't do it, do have an internal cloud provider, do be a customer of the cloud, do eliminate all internal IaaS, and so on.
- **"Cloud adoption eliminates all internal IT."** This is not true. Even with an aggressive strategy of externalizing, there can still be a brokering role for

IT departments to help with the business contract for cloud providers, as well as to help with the increased demand for security, procurement, data management services, and monitoring.

- **"The IT department can safely ignore the cloud."** This not true. The IT department must understand that cloud computing is so accessible that they no longer enjoy a natural monopoly on IT. If they ignore the cloud, they will be left only with the legacy applications. The IT department is in the best position to be an internal cloud provider, as well as to help the business make better use of external cloud providers.

- **"Data stored in the cloud is not secure."** This is another fiction. Public cloud providers are audited by third parties on a recurring basis and have the expertise and resources to provide better security than most private organizations do.

Cloud computing can be a disruptive technology, much like the PC was in its day. Both technologies initially appealed to the mass market and consumers, rather than corporate customers. As a consequence, when you adopt the cloud, you must start with applications that have high value in the cloud but are not very risky.

For example, rather than first moving a customer transaction application to the cloud, perhaps using office productivity software in the cloud (SaaS) is a better first choice for the following reasons:

- SaaS offerings, such as word processing, spreadsheets, and the like, are mature and designed for stability, security, and delivery to remote users.

- Users can access office productivity software from anywhere using many types of devices, so it is convenient to be productive.

- Users can collaborate easily with data stored in the cloud. For example, a user could store a spreadsheet in the cloud that requires multiple changes from multiple colleagues. Instead of emailing the file to multiple colleagues and then merging all the received changes, many SaaS offerings allow multiuser online editing of data.

exam
ⓦatch

Look for keywords such as complex, proprietary, and mission-critical in exam questions when determining poor candidates for initial cloud pilots. Less critical applications related to general office productivity tend to make better choices in this regard.

Cloud computing is relevant for companies of all sizes, but it does not affect all groups of users and departments equally. Table 4-1 shows how different user groups are affected by cloud computing.

What types of applications and services should be considered for a pilot? Moving applications, servers, or services to the cloud must result in business value. Standard risk management techniques can be used to determine whether the benefits of cloud adoption outweigh potential unwanted outcomes.

Complex applications that are difficult to migrate are not good candidates for cloud adoption. An example of this might be a customized line-of-business application storing data in a nonstandard format.

Mission-critical applications that require the highest level of reliability might be best controlled within an organization's IT infrastructure and not in the cloud. Exceptions to this include e-commerce and IT service providers.

---

e x a m
watch

Organizations using complex or mission-critical applications might have them running on a virtual machine already. If an exam question *suggests migrating a virtual machine running a critical application to the cloud, this could present business value but not as an initial cloud pilot.*

TABLE 4-1 How Cloud Adoption Affects Different User Groups

User or Group	Effect of Cloud Computing
Office workers	These users interact directly with applications delivered to them over the network. The ability to store documents in the cloud facilitates collaboration. The ability to access SaaS apps from anywhere using any device fosters a more productive work environment.
Internal IT departments	Cloud deployment requires IT expertise. IT workers will configure, monitor, and maintain security and cloud service usage policies, as well as be involved in negotiating service level agreement (SLA) details. Local IT staff will also support client devices (desktops, laptops, tablets, and smartphones) and network connectivity.
IT service providers	Public and private cloud providers must provide the elastic, self-provisioned, and on-demand computing infrastructure that characterizes a cloud. Private cloud providers act as an external service provider for business units within the organization.

For example, applications with substantial peak loads are possible candidates because cloud elasticity can save time and money. Application development and testing can also work great in the cloud because virtual machines, database servers, and application components can be used as needed and deprovisioned when not needed. Desktop productivity applications (word processing, spreadsheets, presentations, and email) can simply provide user interfaces for users. Data collaboration is facilitated because data can be stored in a central location, the cloud, where multiple users can access it.

Adopting Service Models

Companies can adopt various cloud service models for their exclusive use; this defines a private cloud.

Private IaaS

One of the paths for adopting the cloud is through private IaaS, which is a private cloud in a manner of speaking, as shown in Figure 4-1. The business benefit of this approach is that it will allow server infrastructure to be deployed much more rapidly, which will speed up test and development projects.

To realize this goal, an initial private cloud can be built. It might even be possible to realize a pilot with existing hardware servers or acquired IT resources, such as a SAN, capacity, or virtual network. It will be important to create a standard-services catalog for this service; otherwise, the desired high level of self-service will not be realized. Users of this type of infrastructure should be subject to cost chargeback, based on an operational metering system.

To control unlimited growth of the number of virtual servers, the best practice is to require every virtual server to have a finite lifetime, after which it will automatically be deleted.

FIGURE 4-1

A private
IaaS cloud

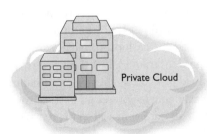

Private Cloud

An IT organization that aims to deliver private IaaS must have substantial competence in server virtualization because that is the underlying technology for IaaS.

Private PaaS

Private PaaS derives its business benefits from making databases that might contain customer or product data, transactions, or statistics available for reuse. By allowing access to a library of functionality on these databases, large organizations can divide responsibility and deploy applications quickly, thus improving time to market. The IT department has the responsibility of ensuring this data is always available.

Private SaaS

Delivering web applications to end users internally is something most organizations have been doing for a long time. Remember that SaaS is defined as delivering productivity software to end users over a network. It should allow users to work remotely anytime, from anywhere, using any type of device. The difference here is the apps are running on company-owned assets.

CERTIFICATION OBJECTIVE 4.02

Cloud Computing Vendor Roles and Capabilities

Adopting cloud computing implies that new relations with new vendors will be developed. Depending on the characteristics of the adopting organization, not every vendor is a good fit.

The cloud consumer (also known as *customer* or *subscriber*) is the person or organization that maintains a business relationship with, and uses service from, cloud providers, according to the NIST.

The cloud carrier connects consumers to the provider's facilities. This could simply be the Internet (public cloud), or it could be a private network (private cloud). In some situations, it makes sense to transport data through physical means (such as hard disks and CDs). This is also a cloud carrier function.

The cloud provider is the person, organization, or entity responsible for making a service available to interested parties: the consumers. This involves owning or contracting all hardware and software assets necessary for delivering the service.

Providers depend on a number of components for their service. The most important ones are as follows:

- **Virtualization software components**   Virtualization is essential for IaaS, PaaS, and SaaS. Self-service web portals for provisioning and deprovisioning virtual machines help manage virtualization, especially with IaaS and PaaS.
- **Software libraries**   PaaS providers maintain and operate software libraries for reuse by other applications. This increases the speed of application development and reduces the time to market.
- **Software packages**   SaaS is packaged software delivered as a service and optimized for remote use by a variety of devices.
- **Management software**   This is software for automating the running of the cloud and provisioning virtual machines. This could be developed by the cloud provider, or it could be third-party software.
- **Service**   Customers can take advantage of self-service where they order their service from a web portal, or customer service can be very elaborate to the point where the provider has dedicated staff for the customer.
- **Broker**   Much like a mortgage broker, cloud brokers find and potentially negotiate the best relationship and SLA between the cloud customer and cloud provider.
- **Auditing**   Auditors conduct an independent assessment of cloud services, information system operations, performance, and security. Frequent third-party audits are one of the reasons public clouds are considered very secure compared to private clouds.

Vendor and Provider Dependencies

Cloud computing creates new dependencies on vendors and service providers. Ownership of some hardware and software assets, as well as control over key design decisions, shifts away from the user to the provider. Vendors differ from service providers in that vendors sell solutions that customers can use even if the vendor goes out of business. Service providers work on a continuous basis.

For cloud services, ownership is more of an issue than it is for hardware and software assets. If a service provider stops operating, the consumer has an immediate problem because access will be dropped instantly. If a supplier of hardware or software goes out of business, there will be some time left to find alternatives. In both cases, an alternative has to be found sooner or later. This is what is called an *exit strategy* out of the relationship with the vendor. Some call this Plan B or, more formally, a contingency plan.

Having a contingency plan is nothing new to IT. IT departments have always had to deal with technology vendors changing direction, as well as with disaster recovery and business continuity planning.

Risk Management

The major risk with external service providers and technology providers is the dependency on them. If the service, hardware, or software is no longer available, this can be damaging to the organization. Proper risk management mandates that the risk is managed or accepted. It is not always necessary to have a completely identical alternative standby; the important thing is that the cost or damage of the risk is acceptable.

Data in Storage at a Service Provider   Businesses cannot run without reliable access to related data. Storing data in the cloud makes it centrally available, but network access to your cloud provider, or the cloud provider going out of business, would render that data inaccessible. The data might consist of the following:

- The data could be your customer database in a CRM application.
- The data could be all the virtual machines you have configured at your IaaS.
- The data could be accumulated by the application. Think of an employee knowledge management system with a lot of contributed articles. It could be hard or costly to re-create that data.

Virtual Machines   A server with an operating system represents value. A server with an operating system and a lot of specifically configured and finely tuned software can represent a lot more value. This is even true if the software is free, open software. In a virtualized environment, this server is nothing more than a large data file. Nevertheless, if these configurations are tailored to a specific provider or virtualization technology, reengineering them for a different platform may be costly.

Software Packages   SaaS providers typically run their own software, rather than licensing it from a software vendor. This makes the potential for software lock-in big. Because SaaS providers typically charge on a pay-per-use basis, there is little software license investment lost when such a provider suspends its service.

However, the data that is stored in the application may not be easily converted to a similar application. In addition, all staff working with the application will have to be retrained—or even have to change their work processes.

Cloud Management Tools   Cloud management tools are indispensable above a certain scale of operation. The vendors of these tools claim that the tools will help in migrating applications from one cloud to another, thus reducing the lock-in risk. Yet, they do so at the expense of locking you in to their particular management tool.

on the job

Because the dependency on a cloud provider is so great, be sure to have a contingency plan in case your provider is no longer available. You might have important data and virtual machines stored in the cloud. Make sure this data can be exported or backed up elsewhere and used in a "Plan B" provider solution, or consider hosting these resources on your own servers if a provider fails.

CERTIFICATION OBJECTIVE 4.03

Organizational Capabilities That Are Relevant for Realizing Cloud Benefits

Once organizations have made their strategic choices with respect to their place in the IT and cloud value chain, the necessary next step is adapting the operating model of the IT function, as shown in Figure 4-2. This operating model shows the processes, organization, and technology needed to support the business vision.

FIGURE 4-2

IT operating model and cloud adoption

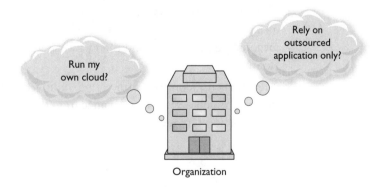

An important strategic choice for an organization is whether it wants to run its own cloud. Running your own cloud implies choices for virtualization technology, a systems management platform, and a skill set for people, as well as an extensive set of IT service management processes.

Another alternative could be to rely on outsourced applications only. This may be an appropriate choice for a small business or a department within a larger organization. Still, a vision has to be developed with respect to SaaS vendors and the way to select them. The consequence of this choice is that the number of technical skills required is more limited.

Regardless of the strategic choices made with respect to cloud computing, the IT department has to learn to work with managing shared infrastructures, whether private or public, and has to learn to provision services, rather than servers. There are also likely to be changes in the way applications are derived from business needs, selected, implemented, operated, and decommissioned.

Organization Roles and Skills

Depending on the vision and operating model selected, roles and skills might change. Cloud computing is a developing area. The cloud ecosystem is evolving and business requirements are changing, and the required roles and skills will change as well.

- An important skill is being able to articulate the business value that cloud computing can bring, for example, by enabling more collaborative work processes both inside and outside the organization.

- In a cloud-enabled world, there is a greater opportunity to modularize applications into reusable components and integrate them with other data sources. This is what is called *service-oriented architecture*.

- Technologies, such as virtualization, IaaS, SaaS, and PaaS, need to be understood in order to evaluate their applicability.

- Selection and procurement services become important skills. This includes mapping the requirements of service level agreements (SLAs) to offerings, negotiating those SLAs and their parameters, and managing the SLA and contract.

- Measurement, monitoring, metering, billing, and reporting form an important skill set, which derives its relevance from the existence of shared and potentially externalized resources.

- When costs become more variable and more opportunities for trade-offs between capital and operational expenditures appear, financial engineering becomes a relevant skill set. This will help in cost optimization as well as proper chargeback.
- Security, access protection, and risk management in the cloud are not particularly harder in the cloud, just different.

Because new and different skills are required to ensure the successful adoption of a cloud strategy, new career opportunities evolve as a result. Some of the job roles will already exist, but cloud adoption will change how those roles are performed.

IT has traditionally provisioned solutions that meet business needs. With both public and private cloud solutions, self-provisioning allows quicker access to computing resources. Private clouds mean that IT must ensure the appropriate cloud fabric is in place to allow self-provisioning.

Adopting the appropriate level of cloud computing requires a number of steps to be undertaken. These steps are the critical success factors:

1. The organization must develop a vision of the way cloud benefits are realized. This vision must be derived from the strategy of the organization and aligned with the important stakeholders. Without this vision, any subsequent elaboration will diverge and become counterproductive.

2. The appropriate operating model for the vision must be designed. The operating model is a blueprint for the way IT is organized. Without this model, it will be hard to develop processes that will work across the entire organization.

3. The vision embodied in the operating model must be executed. Priorities must be established in order to move from the vision to things that actually work.

4. The results of these steps must be regularly evaluated, and this evaluation must be acted upon. Items that must be periodically evaluated include the following:
   - Cloud solutions must be monitored to determine their efficiency and effectiveness.
   - Cloud adoption usually means that IT services are coupled with specific business processes.
   - The cloud benefits must outweigh the cloud-related risks and expenditures.

Migrating Applications to the Cloud

The choices available when you move to the cloud mirror the choices available in a cloud exit strategy of the sort we described earlier. Here are a few examples of the range available:

■ Move the entire application stack to an IaaS provider, replacing the existing servers.

■ Replace the application by a functionally equivalent application in the cloud, which is a SaaS approach.

■ Adopt an intermediate median strategy, where the application is broken into pieces, and each of these pieces is separately considered for migration to a cloud. This creates interfaces between application components that could be reused as PaaS components.

Each alternative has to be weighed against the business reason for cloud adoption. For example, a cost reduction goal might favor a SaaS approach, whereas a scalability goal is more likely to lead to a PaaS approach, because the breakup will enable more scalability in each component.

CERTIFICATION SUMMARY

Choosing the right cloud solution for a specific business can be difficult. Initial cloud testing should be done with low-risk applications that are not critical to business functions; this is usually a SaaS offering such as word processing. Cloud elasticity makes applications with unpredictable peak loads excellent cloud candidates.

Where office staff might be affected by SaaS offerings, an organization's IT department would be involved in selecting and testing cloud services, as well as ensuring reliable network connections to cloud providers.

Private cloud offerings are for the exclusive use of a single organization. This type of cloud would run on company-owned computing hardware.

Cloud providers offer their IT services by way of virtualization, which enables rapid cloud elasticity. The hardware and software required to deliver these services are the concern of the provider, not the cloud customer. A web-based management interface is provided for cloud customers to add or remove cloud offerings as needed.

Because public cloud services are not exclusively controlled by the organization using its services, there are inherent risks. Losing network connectivity to the cloud vendor means losing access to cloud software and data. The same is true if a cloud provider goes out of business. These risks must be assessed and managed accordingly.

Successful cloud adoption requires a change to some organizational roles as well as the ongoing reassessment of cloud computing. Skills such as selecting cloud services that provide business value and selecting or negotiating SLAs that map to business objectives represent roles that may have had limited impact previously. Monitoring cloud services on an ongoing basis is crucial to evaluating effectiveness.

Moving applications to the cloud might involve migrating existing on-premises virtual machines to a cloud provider or building new virtual machines in the cloud. For SaaS, selecting a new yet functionally similar product can be an effective strategy.

✓ TWO-MINUTE DRILL

Typical Steps Leading to Successful Cloud Adoption

❑ Pilot low-risk applications in the cloud rather than mission-critical or complex applications.

❑ Applications whose data requires collaboration can benefit from cloud storage.

❑ Internal IT staffers are involved in evaluating cloud solutions and application migration as well as monitoring cloud deployments.

❑ Multiple cloud providers should be evaluated to find the best fit that meets the business needs.

❑ For larger organizations, a private cloud might offer better solutions than a public cloud.

Cloud Computing Vendor Roles and Capabilities

❑ Cloud consumers (subscribers) use the services offered by cloud providers.

❑ Cloud carriers provide connectivity between the cloud subscriber and the cloud provider.

❑ The service offerings of providers include virtualization, software libraries, software packages, self-service portals, and management portals.

❑ Cloud services work only if the network is available. Redundant network connections, local in-house application hosting, and additional cloud providers might be components of a contingency plan.

Organizational Capabilities That Are Relevant for Realizing Cloud Benefits

❑ Internal IT staff responsibilities will shift from provisioning on-premises servers to provisioning scalable cloud services.

❑ Internal IT staff must monitor the performance and reliability of cloud services.

❑ Modularizing applications into reusable components makes applications quicker to develop and increases their life span.

❑ Selecting the appropriate cloud services that increase business value and negotiating the related SLAs (if possible) are critical skills.

Migrating Applications to the Cloud

❑ An organization's on-premises servers might be migrated to virtual machines in the cloud.

❑ Replacing an application with a functional cloud equivalent might facilitate the adoption of a cloud solution.

❑ Complex applications can be broken into smaller reusable cloud components that can be migrated separately from one another.

SELF TEST

The following questions will help you measure your understanding of the material presented in this chapter. Read all the choices carefully because there might be more than one correct answer.

Typical Steps Leading to Successful Cloud Adoption

1. Which types of applications would be good cloud pilot candidates? (Choose two.)
   A. Custom line-of-business software requiring high availability
   B. An employee knowledge base application with unpredictable peak loads
   C. Spreadsheets requiring multiple simultaneous user updates
   D. Payroll application that stores data in a proprietary format

2. Which of the following is not a consideration when planning IaaS adoption?
   A. Cloud provider application development tools
   B. Reduced time to deploy new servers
   C. OPEX versus CAPEX
   D. Ability to remove unneeded servers

Cloud Computing Vendor Roles and Capabilities

3. What must be adhered to when your chosen cloud provider ceases to exist?
   A. Disaster recovery plan
   B. Exit strategy
   C. Virtualization
   D. Mission statement

4. Which of the following risks must be assessed when considering cloud adoption?
   A. Weak security provided by public cloud providers
   B. Loss of network connectivity
   C. Failed virtual servers
   D. Lack of on-demand growth capacity

Organizational Capabilities That Are Relevant for Realizing Cloud Benefits

5. Which of the following skills will internal IT require when adopting a cloud solution?
   A. Performance monitoring
   B. Security auditing
   C. Configuring network routers
   D. Writing scripts to automate virtual machine deployment

6. Which IT process might be affected by cloud adoption?
   A. Financial management
   B. Budget projections
   C. Personnel management
   D. Capacity management

Migrating Applications to the Cloud

7. When evaluating the migration of one of your applications to the cloud, you discover complexities that may make migration impossible. In this case, what strategy might you employ?
   A. Find a functionally equivalent cloud application.
   B. Migrate the application to the cloud anyway.
   C. Export application data, provision a new virtual machine in the cloud, and then import application data to the new virtual machine.
   D. Export application data, provision a new physical machine in the cloud, and then import application data to the new physical machine.

8. What business benefit is realized by migrating an application to the cloud?
   A. Stronger data encryption
   B. Less risk when there is a loss of network connectivity
   C. Ability to quickly scale in response to business needs
   D. Greater variety in virtual machine operating systems

SELF TEST ANSWERS

Typical Steps Leading to Successful Cloud Adoption

1. Which types of applications would be good cloud pilot candidates? (Choose two.)
   A. Custom line-of-business software requiring high availability
   B. An employee knowledge base application with unpredictable peak loads
   C. Spreadsheets requiring multiple simultaneous user updates
   D. Payroll application that stores data in a proprietary format

   ☑ **B and C.** Cloud elasticity lends itself to provisioning services with variable peak loads. Data collaboration for cloud-stored data, such as spreadsheets, is commonplace with SaaS solutions.
   ☒ **A and D** are incorrect. Custom software might be difficult to migrate to the cloud. Even though some cloud solutions offer high availability, the combination of custom software and high availability makes this a poor cloud pilot candidate. Proprietary data formats can also present complexities when migrating that data to the cloud, so this too is a poor choice.

2. Which of the following is not a consideration when planning IaaS adoption?
   A. Cloud provider application development tools
   B. Reduced time to deploy new servers
   C. OPEX versus CAPEX
   D. Ability to remove unneeded servers

   ☑ **A.** Application development tools are related to PaaS, not IaaS.
   ☒ **B, C,** and **D** are incorrect. Each of the listed items is a valid consideration when planning IaaS adoption.

Cloud Computing Vendor Roles and Capabilities

3. What must be adhered to when your chosen cloud provider ceases to exist?
   A. Disaster recovery plan
   B. Exit strategy
   C. Virtualization
   D. Mission statement

☑ **B.** A preplanned exit strategy will define actions to be taken should a cloud provider no longer be available.

☒ **A, C,** and **D** are incorrect. Disaster recovery plans and virtualization are inherent parts of today's cloud computing environment when the cloud provider is functioning. Mission statements are not related to whether a cloud provider is available.

4. Which of the following risks must be assessed when considering cloud adoption?
   A. Weak security provided by public cloud providers
   B. Loss of network connectivity
   C. Failed virtual servers
   D. Lack of on-demand growth capacity

☑ **B.** Without network connectivity to cloud services, virtual servers, data, and cloud applications are unavailable. This possibility must be assessed to determine whether the risk is acceptable.

☒ **A, C,** and **D.** Public cloud providers have the requirement, resources, and expertise to exercise a higher degree of security than most organizations could do themselves. Failed virtual servers present a risk whether they are hosted by the organization or a cloud provider. High availability (clustering) and backups minimize downtime. On-demand provisioning of cloud services is one of the reasons organizations seek to adopt cloud solutions; it is not a risk.

Organizational Capabilities That Are Relevant for Realizing Cloud Benefits

5. Which of the following skills will internal IT require when adopting a cloud solution?
   A. Performance monitoring
   B. Security auditing
   C. Configuring network routers
   D. Writing scripts to automate virtual machine deployment

☑ **A.** Adopting a cloud solution means monitoring the performance of the solution on an ongoing basis to ensure the solution presents business value.

☒ **B, C,** and **D.** Security auditing is the cloud provider's concern, not the cloud consumer, as are configuring network routers and presenting the tools for virtual machine deployment.

6. Which IT process might be affected by cloud adoption?

A. Financial management

B. Budget projections

C. Personnel management

D. Capacity management

☑ **D.** Capacity planning and management might be affected with cloud adoption. Determining how many virtual machines, how much storage, or how many user mail accounts are required are examples of how this IT process might be affected.

☒ **A, B,** and **C** are incorrect because they are not IT processes.

Migrating Applications to the Cloud

7. When evaluating the migration of one of your applications to the cloud, you discover complexities that may make migration impossible. In this case, what strategy might you employ?

A. Find a functionally equivalent cloud application.

B. Migrate the application to the cloud anyway.

C. Export application data, provision a new virtual machine in the cloud, and then import application data to the new virtual machine.

D. Export application data, provision a new physical machine in the cloud, and then import application data to the new physical machine.

☑ **A.** Sometimes specific commercial applications that run well within an organization are not available in the cloud. Often there are functionally equivalences offered by cloud providers; this should be researched by internal IT staff.

☒ **B, C,** and **D** are incorrect because the question states that there are complexities impeding migration to the cloud.

8. What business benefit is realized by migrating an application to the cloud?
   A. Stronger data encryption
   B. Less risk when there is a loss of network connectivity
   C. Ability to quickly scale in response to business needs
   D. Greater variety in virtual machine operating systems

☑   **C.** Moving an application to the cloud must have business value. Cloud elasticity allows a quick response to unpredictable business demands that use computing resources.

☒   **A, B,** and **D** are incorrect. Strong data encryption is possible without migrating an application to the cloud. Loss of network connectivity is a major risk that must be properly assessed. The cloud does not prevent a greater variety in virtual machine operating systems than could be made available within an organization.

5

Operating Cloud Computing

C loud computing changes IT service management within an organization. More work is done by external suppliers, which means the structure of a business has to change. In some cases, current internal staff within an organization will have their job roles redefined, while in other cases new job roles will be created. Some roles will be eliminated, because they no longer provide substantial value in a cloud environment.

Implementing cloud services means the demand for computer resources is more quickly met and resources can be self-provisioned by those needing them. These outcomes—increased flexibility and quicker access to tools—result in greater efficiency, but internal service management processes will need to change to accommodate these quickened demands.

CERTIFICATION OBJECTIVE 5.01

Cloud Computing Changes on IT Service Management

Cloud computing is a set of technologies and an approach to IT service delivery, but no technology exists in a business without a set of procedures and standards to guide its operation and management. IT staff members work together to carry out the processes that deliver the IT services on which a business relies. It is the nature of these processes to be closely interrelated. You cannot change one process without making compensatory changes in other processes. Changes in one process impact one or more other processes and may require compensatory changes to ensure continued smooth operations. An organization could make changes to process A without making compensatory changes to process B, but there is risk in that approach.

Impact on Service Management Processes

Cloud adoption is motivated by business benefits, and implementing cloud computing means that some processes must change. Not all organizations have the same business reasons for cloud adoption; hence, organizations might also differ in their focus on the service management processes that need adapting first.

The traditional IT model involves acquiring, installing, and maintaining computing resources that provide business value. This takes time (loss of time means loss of a competitive edge) and a larger initial investment than "pay-as-you-go" cloud services, where you are essentially renting computing services. Cloud computing introduces an elastic, quickly provisioned service consumption model. This reduced time frame means IT processes must change.

Service reliability becomes a focal point instead of traditional computing resource availability. For example, computing resources are readily available in a public cloud, whereas within an organization they are limited. Because cloud services are accessible across a network, the cloud provider and your network connection to them must be reliable.

Service Management Phases

Cloud services require changes to some processes within each of the four service management phases. These processes will be discussed in greater detail in the following sections.

The ITIL life cycle consists of four common IT service management phases we will correlate to cloud computing:

- Service Strategy
- Service Design
- Service Operation
- Service Transition

Service Strategy   Managing service levels is a critical part of adopting cloud computing. Because capacity becomes elastic, there is no longer a hard limit on its usage. This is good for performance but potentially bad for cost. As a result, service level agreements with providers take an entirely new shape. With this in mind, the following are some important questions to answer when reviewing service level agreements:

- How elastic is the capacity?
- Can the provider deny you a capacity increase?
- Does the provider have any guarantees on the upper limit?
- How well can you cap or limit usage (ensuring costs cannot exceed a specified dollar amount)?
- How is capacity scaled back when no longer needed?

Remember at all times that with cloud computing the cost base will be much more variable. Traditional chargeback models may change because of the speed at which cloud computing services can be provisioned and deprovisioned. The more you automate the processes around dynamic resource allocation and sharing, the more productive and efficient they will become.

Service Design   Cloud adoption introduces new IT services that can be rapidly provisioned using self-service web portals. Existing IT services in the organization can sometimes be integrated with cloud offerings, thus improving an existing service. For example, your company might host employee email accounts on local mail servers, but before mail arrives on premises, virus scanning and spam filtering are done through a cloud provider service. Cloud services must be monitored to ensure performance is optimal, as shown in Figure 5-1.

Service Operation   Cloud computing often makes one part of a request fulfillment process quicker—for instance, it eliminates a long wait for hardware to be installed—but other parts of the process remain manual and take a long time, such as security entitlements.

Service Transition   In the old days, any IT service change was the end result of a fairly long, manual process. Examples include acquiring new end-user software or new server hardware. As a result, the configuration management database (CMDB)

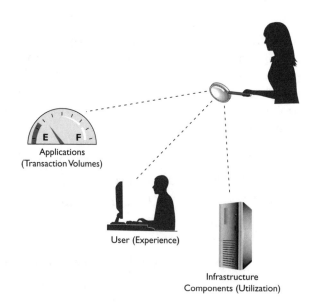

FIGURE 5-1

Monitoring applications and infrastructure to ensure a positive user experience

Applications
(Transaction Volumes)

User (Experience)

Infrastructure
Components (Utilization)

could be reasonably up to date since these things took time. CMDB is a repository of IT services and the underlying components and processes used to deliver them. It connects configuration items to the value they provide to customers. With cloud computing, entities such as servers, workstations, and application installations can come and go much more quickly, so keeping the CMDB up to date is important.

Attributes of some CMDB configuration items (CIs) might change. For example, it makes little sense to know the building location of a virtual server. The service catalog is a list of operational services available for use by users. Because of rapid elasticity, the CMDB may need tighter integration with the service catalog so that the catalog is always up to date. Figure 5-2 lists data that is documented in the CMDB.

FIGURE 5-2

The configuration management database stores data related to IT processes.

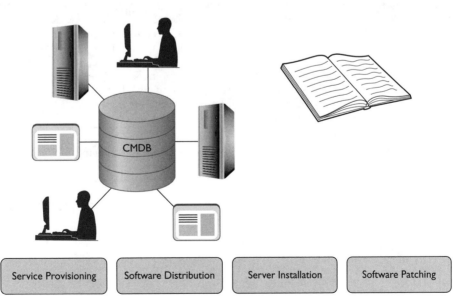

CERTIFICATION OBJECTIVE 5.02

Explore the Potential Impact of Cloud Computing Using ITIL

The Information Technology Infrastructure Library (ITIL) is a widely practiced service management model that ensures IT services are serving business needs, and for the CLO-001 exam you must understand the relationship between ITIL and the IT service changes brought about by cloud computing.

Table 5-1 through Table 5-4 describe potential service changes as they relate to each ITIL life-cycle phase.

on the job

Self-service web portals allow users to quickly provision services such as a new virtual web server needed for an upcoming marketing campaign. Software distribution including patching is maintained by the cloud provider; local IT is no longer responsible for testing, deploying, and monitoring new software installations and updates. Take note that local IT staff should be monitoring the use of cloud services to ensure that the performance and availability align with the SLA, which in turn meets business needs.

TABLE 5-1	How Cloud Adoption Might Change IT Processes Related to the Service Strategy Phase

Process	Description	To Think About
Demand Management	Activities that understand and influence customer demand for services and the provision of capacity to meet those demands. At a strategic level, Demand Management can involve an analysis of the patterns of business activity and user profiles. At a tactical level, it can involve the use of differential charging to encourage customers to use IT services at less busy times.	How do we keep users from ordering too many diverging cloud computing services and creating a management nightmare?
Financial Management	The function and processes responsible for managing an IT service provider's budgeting, accounting, and charging requirements.	How does the end-to-end process of setting strategic and operational targets change? How does chargeback change?

TABLE 5-2	How Cloud Adoption Might Change IT Processes Related to the Service Design Phase	
Process	**Description**	**To Think About**
Service Level Management	The process responsible for negotiating service level agreements (SLAs) and ensuring that they are met. Service Level Management (SLM) is responsible for ensuring that all IT service management processes, operational level agreements (OLAs), and underpinning contracts are appropriate for the agreed service level targets. SLM monitors and reports on service levels and holds regular customer reviews.	What is the internal supply chain for cloud computing? How will it change from today?
Capacity Management	The process responsible for ensuring that the capacity of IT services and IT infrastructure is able to deliver the agreed service level targets in a cost-effective and timely manner. Capacity Management considers all resources required to deliver the IT service and plans for short-, medium-, and long-term business requirements.	What changes happen to Capacity Management when services live in an elastic cloud?
Availability and Service Continuity Management	The process responsible for managing risks that could seriously impact IT services. IT Service Continuity Management (ITSCM) ensures that the IT service provider can always provide the minimum, agreed service levels by reducing the risks to an acceptable level and planning for the recovery of IT services. ITSCM should be designed to support business continuity management.	What opportunities does cloud computing provide for business continuity and high availability?
Information Security Management	The process that ensures the confidentiality, integrity, and availability of an organization's assets, information, data, and IT services. Information Security Management usually forms part of an organizational approach to security management, which has a wider scope than the IT service provider and includes the handling of paper, building access, and phone calls for the entire organization.	What regulations apply to data location? How are user identities in the cloud managed?

exam
ⓦatch

The CLO-001 exam is sure to test your knowledge of which IT processes will change with cloud adoption. Make sure you know the names of the IT processes, how they might change, and which service management phase they belong to.

TABLE 5-3	How Cloud Adoption Might Change IT Processes Related to the Service Operation Phase	
Process	**Description**	**To Think About**
Request Fulfillment	The process responsible for managing the life cycle of all service requests.	How can requests be fulfilled in a self-service way and also be orchestrated across multiple service providers?
Incident Management	The process responsible for managing the life cycle of all incidents. The primary objective of Incident Management is to return the IT service to users as quickly as possible.	What new sources of incidents can we have in a cloud environment? How do we trace their impact to business applications?
Access Management	The process responsible for allowing users to use IT services, data, or other assets. Access Management helps protect the confidentiality, integrity, and availability of assets by ensuring that only authorized users are able to access or modify the assets. Access Management is sometimes referred to as Rights Management or Identity Management.	How do we keep access provisioning from becoming onerous, when assets such as servers come and go very quickly and services reconfigure rapidly? How do we synchronize identities and access across multiple service providers?

TABLE 5-4	How Cloud Adoption Might Change IT Processes Related to the Service Transition Phase	
Process	**Description**	**To Think About**
Change Management	The process responsible for controlling the life cycle of all changes. The primary objective of Change Management is to enable beneficial changes to be made, with minimum disruption to IT services.	How do we make sure that we get change approval from all parties that will be affected in a dynamic, virtual, and elastic environment?
Service Asset and Configuration Management	The process responsible for both Configuration Management and Asset Management.	What are the assumptions built into these processes about how quickly change happens?
Knowledge Management	The process responsible for gathering, analyzing, storing, and sharing knowledge and information within an organization. The primary purpose of Knowledge Management is to improve efficiency by reducing the need to rediscover knowledge.	What new information will we need to capture about cloud computing?
Deployment, Decommission, and Transfer	The activity responsible for the movement of new or changed hardware, software, documentation, processes, and so on, to the live environment. Deployment is part of the Release and Deployment Management process.	How automated are these processes today? How many steps are in the process?

CERTIFICATION SUMMARY

This chapter focused on how cloud adoption can change how IT processes are managed within an organization. ITIL is a common framework used to ensure IT processes map to business needs, thus providing business value.

The first ITIL service management phase is Service Strategy, and cloud adoption introduces new considerations such how cloud elasticity can be best used to meet variable business workloads. Costs might be managed by encouraging the use of cloud services at less busy times or by setting a ceiling dollar amount that cannot be exceeded.

The second ITIL service management phase is Service Design. The cloud provider SLA can sometimes be negotiated so that it aligns with the needs of the business. Capacity Management (storage, virtual machines) is important in meeting the terms in the SLA, as are information security and high availability of IT services.

Service Operation is the third ITIL phase affected by cloud adoption. Self-service is a cloud characteristic that allows the self-provisioning of cloud services, such as the creation of new virtual servers, from a web portal. Cloud customers are charged a fee based on how many virtual machines they create and how each virtual machine is configured in terms of virtual CPUs, memory (RAM), and disk space. When there are disruptions to cloud services, Incident Management details how to restore IT services as quickly as possible. Local IT staff within an organization will be involved with controlling access to cloud services and cloud data for their users.

The final ITIL phase affected by cloud computing is Service Transition. Cloud customers might consider when it is appropriate to move applications and servers from on premises to the cloud or to select new cloud services that mimic the functionality of in-house systems.

✓ TWO-MINUTE DRILL

Cloud Computing Changes on IT Service Management

- ❑ Cloud adoption means that some of your internal IT processes will change.
- ❑ Different organizations will have different IT process changes.
- ❑ The speed with which computing services can be provisioned necessitates changes compared to the traditional method of planning, purchasing, installing, and maintaining IT systems.
- ❑ Instead of ensuring servers, disk space, web sites, and other infrastructure are readily available to users (this is the responsibility of cloud providers), IT staff will ensure cloud services are available and reliable through performance monitoring.
- ❑ Service Strategy, Service Design, Service Operation, and Service Transition are typical service management phases affected by cloud computing.
- ❑ While some IT processes will change significantly, others, such as security entitlements, might not. Users must still be given access to aspects of cloud services related to their job roles.

Explore the Potential Impact of Cloud Computing Using ITIL

- ❑ ITIL maps IT processes to business needs.
- ❑ The use of cloud services demands changes in IT processes in each service management phase.
  - ❑ **Service Strategy Phase**   Demand Management, Service Portfolio Management, and Financial Management are processes that will change. For example, Demand Management relates to how cloud customers can quickly appropriate new computing resources and how these demands can be efficiently met.
  - ❑ **Service Design Phase**   Service Catalog Management, Service Level Management, Supplier Management, Capacity Management, Availability and Service Continuity Management, and Information Security Management are processes impacted by cloud adoption. A good example is Capacity Management; IT services must be available, according to SLA metrics, in a timely manner and at a low cost.

❑ **Service Operation Phase** Request Fulfillment, Event Management, Incident Management, Problem Management, and Access Management must change for a successful cloud implementation. Consider, as an example, that Incident Management includes making sure that cloud IT services are always available to users.

❑ **Service Transition Phase** Change Management, Service Asset and Configuration Management, Knowledge Management, and Deploy, Decommission, and Transfer are processes that must adapt to a cloud environment. For example, with Change Management processes such as Software Distribution, the responsibility for this falls on the cloud provider, where traditionally internal IT staff handled this.

SELF TEST

The following questions will help you measure your understanding of the material presented in this chapter. Read all the choices carefully because there might be more than one correct answer.

Cloud Computing Changes on IT Service Management

1. While evaluating cloud providers, you consider which SLA metrics might require negotiation. Which service management phase does this apply to?
   A. Service Strategy
   B. Service Design
   C. Service Operation
   D. Service Transition

2. One benefit of cloud computing is the ability to quickly procure IT computing resources. Which service management phase does this apply to?
   A. Service Strategy
   B. Service Design
   C. Service Operation
   D. Service Transition

3. Which of the following are reasons IT processes will change with cloud adoption? (Choose two.)
   A. Rapid elasticity
   B. More focus on software patching within an organization's IT department
   C. Less focus on software patching within an organization's IT department
   D. Less focus on cloud service performance

4. Which of the following statements regarding cloud computing is true?
   A. The cloud customer IT staff will no longer be responsible for giving security permissions to users.
   B. Performance monitoring is the sole responsibility of the cloud provider.
   C. Cloud service costs are fixed.
   D. Performance monitoring should be performed by the cloud customer's IT staff.

Explore the Potential Impact of Cloud Computing Using ITIL

5. What obstacle might an organization face related to Demand Management?
   A. Inability to provide enough computing infrastructure
   B. Lack of data security in public clouds
   C. Inability to rapidly deprovision compute resources
   D. Ability of users to access SaaS applications from anywhere

6. How would cloud adoption impact the Service Design phase?
   A. Ensuring SLA metrics are honored.
   B. Fulfilling self-service requests.
   C. Providing confidentiality for sensitive data stored in the cloud.
   D. The CMDB will need to be updated more frequently.

7. Which of the following items directly relate to Change Management?
   A. Negotiating SLA details
   B. Meeting demand for IT services
   C. Installing new software
   D. Ensuring cloud services are always available

8. Access Management is affected by which aspect of cloud computing?
   A. Identity federation
   B. Cloud backup
   C. Network connectivity to the cloud provider
   D. Virtualization

SELF TEST ANSWERS

Cloud Computing Changes on IT Service Management

1. While evaluating cloud providers, you consider which SLA metrics might require negotiation. Which service management phase does this apply to?
   A. Service Strategy
   B. Service Design
   C. Service Operation
   D. Service Transition

   ☑ **B.** The Service Design phase includes making sure the negotiated SLA meets service level targets.
   ☒ **A, C,** and **D** are incorrect. The Service Strategy phase relates more to Demand Management and Financial Management. Service Operation relates to the management of IT service life cycles, once in operation. Service Transition relates to changes in IT service life cycles.

2. One benefit of cloud computing is the ability to quickly procure IT computing resources. Which service management phase does this apply to?
   A. Service Strategy
   B. Service Design
   C. Service Operation
   D. Service Transition

   ☑ **A.** Service Strategy relates to IT processes such as Demand Management. The ease with which users can self-provision resources warrants attention here.
   ☒ **B, C,** and **D** are incorrect. The Service Design phase relates more to SLA Planning and Capacity Management. Service Operation relates to the management of IT service life cycles, once in operation. Service Transition relates to changes in IT service life cycles.

3. Which of the following are reasons IT processes will change with cloud adoption? (Choose two.)
   A. Rapid elasticity
   B. More focus on software patching within an organization's IT department
   C. Less focus on software patching within an organization's IT department
   D. Less focus on cloud service performance

☑   **A** and **C.** Rapid elasticity means it is easier for users to request new or additional IT services; Demand Management takes on new meaning with this. With SaaS, an organization's IT department is not responsible for patching software with updates; this is the cloud provider's responsibility.

☒   **B** and **D** are incorrect. The cloud provider takes care of software patching for cloud services, not the organization's IT department. With cloud adoption, there is an emphasis on monitoring the performance of cloud services; this is something the cloud customer's IT staff can monitor.

4. Which of the following statements regarding cloud computing is true?
    A. The cloud customer IT staff will no longer be responsible for giving security permissions to users.
    B. Performance monitoring is the sole responsibility of the cloud provider.
    C. Cloud service costs are fixed.
    D. Performance monitoring should be performed by the cloud customer's IT staff.

☑   **D.** The cloud customer IT staff should be monitoring cloud service performance to ensure, according to the SLA, business requirements are being met.

☒   **A, B,** and **C.** None of these options is true. Cloud customer IT staff will still be granting access to cloud services to users. Performance monitoring is an important task for the cloud customer. Cloud service costs are normally variable, depending on requested services.

Explore the Potential Impact of Cloud Computing Using ITIL

5. What obstacle might an organization face related to Demand Management?
    A. Inability to provide enough computing infrastructure
    B. Lack of data security in public clouds
    C. Inability to rapidly deprovision compute resources
    D. Ability of users to access SaaS applications from anywhere

☑   **A.** The ability of users to quickly provision computing services not only requires careful attention to computing infrastructure capacity and availability but also suggests capping how many services users can self-provision.

☒   **B, C,** and **D.** Public cloud data security is considered superior to the data security provided by a single organization. The ability of users to rapidly deprovision computing services is seen as a benefit, not an obstacle. Accessing SaaS applications from anywhere is considered a benefit of cloud computing.

6. How would cloud adoption impact the Service Design phase?
- **A.** Ensuring SLA metrics are honored.
- **B.** Fulfilling self-service requests.
- **C.** Providing confidentiality for sensitive data stored in the cloud.
- **D.** The CMDB will need to be updated more frequently.

   ☑   **A.** Service Level Management is an IT process related to the Service Design phase. SLAs must be carefully negotiated, and adherence (by the cloud provider) must be monitored.
   ☒   **B, C,** and **D** are incorrect. Fulfilling self-service requests and cloud data confidentially would impact the Service Operation phase. The Service Transition phase would involve ensuring the CMDB is updated more frequently to match the rapid provisioning and deprovisioning of cloud services.

7. Which of the following items directly relate to Change Management?
- **A.** Negotiating SLA details
- **B.** Meeting demand for IT services
- **C.** Installing new software
- **D.** Ensuring cloud services are always available

   ☑   **C.** Installing software falls under the IT process of Change Management. With SaaS, this is one process where a cloud customer's IT staff will have less work to do since the cloud provider takes care of making software available and patching it.
   ☒   **A, B,** and **D** are not related to Change Management. SLAs relate to Service Level Management, the demand for IT services applies to Demand Management, and cloud service availability applies to Availability and Service Continuity Management.

8. Access Management is affected by which aspect of cloud computing?
- **A.** Identity federation
- **B.** Cloud backup
- **C.** Network connectivity to the cloud provider
- **D.** Virtualization

   ☑   **A.** Identity federation allows a central identity store to be used both inside and outside of an organization. For example, Company A's user accounts can be used to gain access to resources in Company A and Company B, as well as Cloud Provider A.
   ☒   **B, C,** and **D** are incorrect since they have nothing to do with Access Management. Cloud backup and dependencies on network connectivity are related to IT Service Continuity Management. Virtualization does affect all IT processes, but identity federation is a better answer.

6

Governing Cloud Computing

T he purpose of governance is to make sure that investments generate value and that risks are mitigated. This is not a new thing brought on by cloud computing; every organization does this in some way. Companies adopt cloud solutions for many reasons such as to facilitate innovation or to quickly provision temporary computing capacity. Because of these and many other reasons, cloud computing introduces new issues related to governance, such as regulatory compliance, which in the past might have been the sole responsibility of an organization but which now include the cloud provider.

Identify Challenges in Integrating Cloud Computing into an Organization's Existing Governance Framework

With or without cloud solutions, organization must adhere to regulations, data privacy laws, data retention laws, tax laws, and so on. IT services offered by the cloud must fit into these regulatory and legal structures, all while offering business value with acceptable risk.

Risk Management

As mentioned in Chapter 4, there are risks that must be considered when adopting a cloud solution. *Risk management* can be defined as the proactive identification, analysis, and control of those risks that can threaten the assets or earning capacity of an enterprise.

Compliance

All organizations have to comply with legal rules, such as industry-specific regulations. This is especially true for large, publicly listed companies. For example, the Payment Card Industry Data Security Standard (PCI DSS) is a compliance standard stipulating that companies involved with customer debit and credit card transactions maintain a secure environment. There are a number of requirements that must be met to achieve PCI compliance; for example, merchants storing credit card information must pass a network vulnerability scan using an approved scanner.

Companies wanting to adhere to these strict compliance standards must use independent auditors, usually annually. Cloud computing is likely to complicate these processes because external service providers control, to varying degrees, data storage and identity management. Identity management is used to authorize individuals to certain IT systems; this is of critical importance to PCI DSS. An organization must know who has access to what, they must be able to ensure only authorized persons can access required data, and auditing must be in place to track the use of this data.

Being in control of your assets also implies that the current state of these assets is well known. This translates to having appropriate change management in place, as well as having accurate inventory and audit trails. Table 6-1 shows cloud computing pros and cons compared to in-house systems management.

Auditing

Organizations must have backup and recovery plans for their IT assets. Assets include business-related data, network infrastructure, exit strategies, and so on. If any of the assets fail, how is service restored? On the surface, the risk of hardware failure appears to be transferred to the cloud provider. However, the service level agreement (SLA) offered by a provider, as pictured in Figure 6-1, may not be adequate for the business.

In some cases, the SLA can be negotiated such that both parties will benefit.

TABLE 6-1   Cloud Computing Pros and Cons

Cloud Computing Pros	Cloud Computing Cons
Using IaaS can be beneficial to your change management processes. Server and software acquisitions, installation, licensing, patching, and upgrades—cloud service providers take care of these so cloud customers don't have to.	Service providers have their own IT service update and release schedules, and this may not coincide with a customer's best interests.
Providers must pass multiple independent audits on a recurring basis.	Network connectivity problems or a provider going out of business presents disruption risk.
Providers have the resources and expertise to exercise strict security principles.	For cloud storage and backup, customers do not have control of this data in the cloud. Compliance to published sets of standards becomes difficult since the cloud customer and provider must work together.

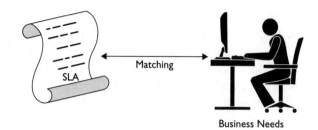

FIGURE 6-1

The provider-supplied SLA may not be acceptable to your organization.

Security

The classic security architecture revolves around a single point of defense that separates company assets from the outside world, that is, the Internet. However, in the cloud computing world, providers will themselves be in this outside world. In addition, it might be necessary to have secure communication between services that are both "in the cloud." In addition, important categories of users might have access to the organization's resources through the public Internet.

Network Security   As a consequence of having multiple providers and users connecting over the Internet, there will be multiple touch points between the organization and the outside world, and it will become necessary to manage multiple distributed firewalls. Some of these firewalls may be operated by your cloud provider to act as a wrapper around there sources that you have established with that provider. A customer would have some limited form of managing this firewall function.

Even though firewalls are important to protect digital assets, they are not all that is required for appropriate security. Using Secure Sockets Layer (SSL) security certificates protects transmitted data between networked computers by encrypting it, but it is sometimes not enough to meet certain standards. PCI DSS certification requires a combination of security mechanisms, not just one such as SSL. Other attack approaches have always existed and will increase in importance as the security technology matures. Such attack approaches include social engineering, cross-site scripting, and so on, and they apply to in-house as well as cloud-based IT.

Social Engineering   *Social engineering* is the act of manipulating people to disclose some kind of confidential information. Examples include the following:

- A hacker posing as IT personnel, calling an unsuspecting end user and asking for their mailbox password before a fictitious weekend mail system upgrade

■ A hacker sending a seemingly authentic mail message with a link to a fraudulent web site where victims might divulge personal data such as banking information

These types of risks exist with both in-house IT system hosting and cloud computing. Cloud customers must be satisfied that cloud provider personnel have completed security training and are not susceptible to social engineering attacks. The key is educating users about these dangerous possibilities.

Cloud Data Storage   One cloud benefit is the ability of authorized persons to access centrally stored data from anywhere to facilitate collaboration. But do you trust your provider to keep your data secure? Encrypting data at rest (stored data versus transmitted data) is an effective means of keeping data private, but because of legal or compliance rules, your data may need to be stored on premises or at a cloud provider within national boundaries. For example, a Canadian company might be required to have their business-related data stored in a data center on Canadian soil under the control of Canadian citizens.

Controlling user access to cloud data differs from controlling user access to on-premises data. User identities, or some form of authenticated user tokens, must be accessible in the cloud to grant access to cloud resources. Possible solutions include replicating on-premises user account information to the cloud or implementing identity federation. Identify federation takes an on-premises authenticated user and represents them as a "security token" to cloud services. The cloud service is configured to trust the on-premises user account provider.

Residual Risks

Assessing and managing risk is a critical component to a successful cloud adoption. There will always be some type of risk, although reduced, even after performing a risk assessment and applying the best solution. Residual risk might result from a technological implementation, but since technology serves business needs, residual risks tend to be more business based.

Most cloud providers have rather extensive security policies and regularly undergo third-party security audits. When considering cloud service providers or comparing them to in-house approaches, you should contrast these policies and procedures with those currently in place. The highest-ranking cloud providers in the industry have published policies and measures that far exceed industry best practices. Any residual risks and measures will have to be addressed by the customer. These residual risks are likely to include the following:

■ The risk that the cloud service provider goes out of business or its service offering deteriorates in quality beyond the acceptable. For these situations, you need an exit plan that describes how data, software, and other digital assets can be moved to a different provider.

■ The risk of government action—especially when the provider is outside your jurisdiction—which may require disclosure of information or denial of service. For example, hardware might be confiscated that hosts both part of your legitimate service as well as an illegal service.

■ The risk that network connectivity between consumers and providers is interrupted or impaired.

Another item to consider is *fate sharing*; one malevolent cloud customer could misuse the cloud infrastructure (for example, sending spam email), which could result in a cloud provider network (which might include your organization) being blacklisted. Assuming your organization uses hosted email, the result would be legitimate mail from within your organization not reaching its destination—a serious impediment.

Service Level Agreement

Services rendered by cloud providers are accompanied by an SLA. Important components of an SLA are a description of the functionality offered, for example, e-mail service; the uptime that is guaranteed, for example, 99.5 percent; the speed with which the service operates, for example, web pages load within two seconds and email is delivered within two minutes; and a financial paragraph that explains the cost structure and penalties. Cloud SLAs might include clauses related to where data will be physically stored and replicated or perhaps which disaster recovery procedures will be followed.

Legal Implications   A service provider executes a number of processes on behalf of the customer, such as accepting logins from users. It might actually also handle identity provisioning. Legal uncertainties can arise around accountability for these processes. Suppose that somebody gains access to the service, without having the right to do so. Who is responsible for any resulting damages? Resolving these issues requires a mixture of technical measures, appropriate auditing and logging, and contractual agreements.

Licensing   With cloud services, traditional licensing models can fail because they are tied to a quantitative measure that is no longer relevant or even desirable.

Often software would have license costs that recurred on a yearly basis tied to the number of CPUs that were installed. When servers are elastically commissioned and decommissioned on an hourly basis, this becomes inconvenient. In recent times, IaaS providers have worked with vendors to tie the licensing cost to metrics that are more practical. For example, the Microsoft Server 2012 operating system has a Datacenter edition that allows an unlimited number of licensed virtual machines running Server 2012; this is a logical approach for a cloud provider.

on the
Job

Enterprise server software licensing is often tied to the number of processors (or processor cores) in the machine. With virtual servers, often the licensing model works similarly in that licensing is tied to the number of virtual processors assigned to the virtual server. When provisioning new virtual servers, some IaaS providers allow you to specify the number of virtual processors—think about how this might affect your software licensing.

CERTIFICATION OBJECTIVE 6.02

Explain the Implications for Direct Cost and Cost Allocations

Traditional IT departments operate on yearly budget cycles. Budgets translate into IT capacity, which under a specific demand translates to a particular business value. The chargeback of IT costs to departments also works in this budget cycle. Elastic IT resources change the basic assumptions of this model. For example, an increase from 10 to 1,000 server equivalents contracted with an IaaS provider, or from 100 users of a SaaS solution to 5,000 users, can happen overnight, so to speak. This "pay-as-you-go" model is incompatible with a yearly budget cycle.

There are a number of possible management measures to consider to reduce the problem of unpredictable cost, for example:

■ Set limits on total cost, which means that any uncertainty in usage can only be downward.

■ Make sure the cost is related to revenue; after all, elastic revenue was probably one of the reasons for having elastic cost.

Another finance- and capacity-related risk is that the success of the application may depend on the possibility that it can scale rapidly. However, there is a risk of service denial from the cloud provider, which may or may not be able to increase the service volume (be it servers, accounts, or whatever) when that need arises. Some providers have facilities to hedge this risk. For a fee, the customer can make reservations of capacity. Generally, without financial commitment from the customer, there is not likely to be much commitment from the provider.

From the viewpoint of a financial controller or chief financial officer, the move from internal IT to public cloud computing represents a reduction of capital on the balance sheet. This might take a while to play out because assets depreciate over the years. Depending on the financial situation of the organization, this reduction of capital may be a good thing.

e x a m

ⓦatch

Capital expenditure (CAPEX) reduction and the increase in operating expenses (OPEX) are sure to show up somehow on the exam. The reduction in CAPEX on IT services allows a business to either save money up front or use that capital to benefit the business in other ways. Bear in mind that the benefit of migrating CAPEX to OPEX might not be realized immediately.

With cloud computing, there is an increased volatility in the cost base. Costs will go up and down more often and more rapidly. This puts greater demand on financial management capabilities.

CERTIFICATION OBJECTIVE 6.03

Understand How to Maintain Strategic Flexibility

From the perspective of the cloud customer, there are clear and present risks such as a provider going out of business or being unavailable across the network. You must have a contingency plan to deal with these potential incidents.

Exit Strategy

One of the fundamental risks in cloud computing is that the vendor either goes out of business (that is, goes bankrupt) or decides to no longer serve the customer well enough. Although this situation is also well known in the context of outsourcing, it can play out much quicker and harsher with cloud computing. This is because of the following:

- A cloud provider can deploy its resources more easily to other clients. A provider of outsourcing has its assets often more dedicated for clients.
- A cloud provider is likely to have a lot more clients, so an individual client is not as important.

When a provider becomes unavailable, as shown in Figure 6-2, it is wise to have a plan for what to do.

FIGURE 6-2

Cloud providers going out of business is a major risk.

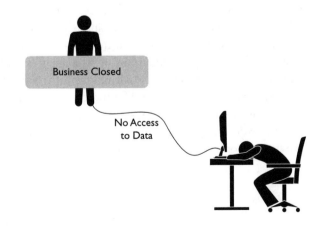

This is called "maintaining strategic flexibility" or having an "exit strategy." This could be done as a component of a business continuity program. Ensuring business continuity is more important than reducing risk.

Strategic Options

Strategic options exist on multiple levels. Understanding vendor dependencies is the first step. The basic structure to follow is to look at business process, application, and infrastructure. You must anticipate future scenarios and build the best possible strategy for each.

These alternatives should be developed in advance, to the extent that it becomes clear what effort is involved in making the move. With that evaluation in hand, it becomes easier to decide which alternative is better and would merit further detailing.

There are considerations that will shape your portfolio of strategic options. When servers stop being available (for example, because an IaaS provider goes out of business), one alternative might be to rehost applications on different servers. This could be done by moving to a different cloud provider, by hosting applications in-house, or by adopting a hybrid cloud solution.

If a cloud provider SaaS offering is no longer available, a functional equivalent may be available by the same provider or another provider, possibly even internal to your organization. If this is the case, consider the data from previously used SaaS solutions and how it can be used with a new SaaS solution. This could require exporting old SaaS data to a standard file format such as comma-separated value (CSV) or Extensible Markup Language (XML) before importing it to a new SaaS system.

An alternative might be to migrate to a different application (probably including migrating the underlying infrastructure). This might also be the strategy if a SaaS provider stops delivering. Business processes that use the application or SaaS solution might be outsourced. An example could be credit card processing.

Cloud providers going out of business does not present the only future possibility that must be considered. Maintaining strategic flexibility includes using the cloud to enhance business processes and ultimately bring value to the business. For example, a business might use their own IT infrastructure during normal business activity levels, but when there are peaks in business activity (which translates to increased IT service demand), cloud IT services (for example, additional virtual servers) are provisioned only when needed during the peak activity.

CERTIFICATION SUMMARY

In this chapter, we began by discussing how cloud adoption introduces changes in how companies adhere to standards. Cloud adoption means companies no longer have full control over all IT resources and services. Complying with regulations or standards such as PCI DSS requires companies to work with their cloud provider to ensure both parties meet their responsibilities. For example, many laws, regulations, and standards require companies to know who has access to which resources, and this access must be audited.

The cloud changes how we think of security. Security risks have always existed with computing solutions, and that also applies to the cloud. Cloud providers might control network firewalls in addition to your organization controlling its firewalls. Encryption of transmitted or stored data is an important component of being compliant with some data security standards. People controlling or using computers must be wary of social engineering, which is the act of tricking people to disclose some kind of confidential information. Not only should employees within an organization understand these dangers, but cloud provider personnel must exercise diligence to mitigate these possibilities.

Risk management must now account for cloud providers doing their part. Even after properly assessing and managing risks, there are sometimes residual risks such as a cloud provider going out of business. Sometimes governments or law enforcement may take action against cloud providers, such as confiscating cloud provider computing equipment used for illegal activities, which can limit business productivity.

Cloud service level agreements are contracts between cloud customers and cloud providers stipulating expected levels of service such as uptime and response time. Where data is physically stored or replicated might be required in an SLA because of government privacy laws.

Cloud customers rent the IT services they need at the time they are needed. Because these costs are variable, limits must be put in place to ensure costs do not skyrocket beyond acceptable limits. Cloud services costs must be periodically reevaluated to ensure the costs are related to generating revenue.

A cloud exit strategy outlines a contingency plan should a cloud provider no longer be available. Examples include using a different cloud provider, hosting IT services in-house, or using a different (yet functionally equivalent) IT service.

✓ TWO-MINUTE DRILL

Identify Challenges in Integrating Cloud Computing into an Organization's Existing Governance Framework

❑ Cloud solutions must fit into regulatory and legal structures.

❑ Risk management prioritizes business continuity.

❑ Compliance standards such as the Sarbanes-Oxley Act (SOA) and Payment Card Industry Data Security Standard (PCI DSS) might be required by organizations; these rules must be followed even if using cloud solutions.

❑ The auditing of in-house IT systems or of cloud provider systems and processes changes with cloud adoption.

❑ Service level agreements (SLAs) must be aligned with business needs.

❑ The legal implications of a provider's failure to meet SLA stated items must be considered.

❑ Cloud network security and data storage security must fit within an acceptable risk framework. Sometimes this is dictated by industry-specific regulations or legislation.

❑ Primary cloud computing risks include cloud providers going out of business or being unreachable across a network, as well as government or law-enforcement action upon a cloud provider.

❑ The licensing of software running in virtual servers may differ from running on physical servers.

Explain the Implications for Direct Cost and Cost Allocations

❑ Yearly budget cycles are not compatible with cloud solutions since cloud solutions can be rapidly provisioned and deprovisioned; new financial management skills must be put into practice.

❑ Because of cost variability with cloud computing, ceiling limits on OPEX can be put in place to control costs.

❑ CAPEX converted to OPEX might not appear to yield benefits right away because of the timeframe over which capital assets are depreciated.

Understand How to Maintain Strategic Flexibility

- ❑ Plan for future undesirable scenarios by coming up with options for each scenario.

- ❑ Exit strategies are contingency plans should a cloud provider become unavailable.

- ❑ Cloud providers going out of business present potential business disruptions that must be planned for.

- ❑ Impediments to network connectivity to cloud providers present another potential business disruption that must be planned for.

- ❑ Hosting IT services with another cloud provider or in-house can maximize business continuity if there are problems with a specific cloud provider.

- ❑ Hybrid cloud solutions (private and public cloud) can augment business continuity and flexible response to business needs; normal business IT workloads might be hosted on a private cloud, and peak business IT workloads could be provisioned as needed in a public cloud.

- ❑ If a provider SaaS solution becomes available, consider a functional equivalent offered by another provider, or consider hosting in-house.

SELF TEST

The following questions will help you measure your understanding of the material presented in this chapter. Read all the choices carefully because there might be more than one correct answer.

Identify Challenges in Integrating Cloud Computing into an Organization's Existing Governance Framework

1. You are negotiating SLA terms with your cloud provider. Your company's chief financial officer, Mia, has concerns with items contained within the SLA. Which item might Mia be interested in?
   A. Cloud service uptime
   B. Switching CAPEX to OPEX
   C. Cloud service termination fees
   D. Web page loading time

2. Which of the following might not be controlled by a public cloud provider?
   A. Cloud service uptime
   B. Web page load time
   C. Cloud service termination fees
   D. Network connection

3. Which of the following cloud-related items presents the greatest risk to business activity for a cloud customer?
   A. Network connectivity problems
   B. Cloud providers going out of business
   C. Inability to encrypt data stored in the cloud
   D. Migrating in-house virtual machines to the cloud

Explain the Implications for Direct Cost and Cost Allocations

4. How does cloud adoption change financial management skills?
   A. Yearly budget cycles change because of rapid cloud elasticity.
   B. Cloud customers must monitor their own cloud resource usage and pay accordingly.
   C. OPEX becomes CAPEX.
   D. Cloud service costs are fixed.
   E. Performance monitoring should be performed by the cloud customer's IT staff.

5. Which of the following statements correctly reflects costs associated with cloud computing?
   A. There is an up-front capital investment.
   B. SLAs never contain cloud service termination fees.
   C. An organization's funds are used to acquire server hardware.
   D. Costs can be volatile.

6. How can unpredictable costs associated with cloud services be managed? (Choose two.)
   A. Choose the cheapest cloud provider.
   B. Set limits on total costs for a given timeframe.
   C. Ensure costs are related to revenue.
   D. Prohibit IaaS from being used.

Understand How to Maintain Strategic Flexibility

7. What should you do to ensure your cloud data can be used with other cloud providers? (Choose two.)
   A. Use the fastest network connection possible.
   B. Know the format in which cloud data is stored.
   C. Know the maximum usable cloud storage capacity.
   D. Know the format cloud data can be exported to.

8. You are planning strategies related to your cloud provider becoming unavailable. Which of the following will ensure business continuity? (Choose two.)
   A. In-house hosting
   B. Cloud backup
   C. Network connectivity to the cloud provider
   D. Using an alternate cloud provider

SELF TEST ANSWERS

Identify Challenges in Integrating Cloud Computing into an Organization's Existing Governance Framework

1. You are negotiating SLA terms with your cloud provider. Your company's chief financial officer, Mia, has concerns with items contained within the SLA. Which item might Mia be interested in?

A. Cloud service uptime
B. Switching CAPEX to OPEX
C. Cloud service termination fees
D. Web page loading time

☑ **C.** Cloud service termination fee terms can be buried in the SLA and must be accounted for as they relate to an exit strategy.

☒ **A, B,** and **D** are incorrect. Cloud service uptime and web page loading time are technical details that would interest the IT department, not the finance people. Switching CAPEX to OPEX is not part of an SLA.

2. Which of the following might not be controlled by a public cloud provider?

A. Cloud service uptime
B. Web page load time
C. Cloud service termination fees
D. Network connection

☑ **D.** The network connection between a cloud customer and a cloud provider is usually controlled by a regional Internet provider.

☒ **A, B,** and **C** are incorrect. Cloud service uptime, web page load time, and cloud service termination fees are controlled by cloud providers, so these items would appear in the SLA.

3. Which of the following cloud-related items presents the greatest risk to business activity for a cloud customer?

A. Network connectivity problems
B. Cloud providers going out of business
C. Inability to encrypt data stored in the cloud
D. Migrating in-house virtual machines to the cloud

☑ **B.** Cloud providers going out of business presents the greatest risk. Even with contingency plans in place, this could be disruptive to an organization, especially if most of the organization's IT services are offered by a single provider.

☒ **A, C,** and **D** are incorrect. Network connectivity problems are a short-term concern. Data encryption and virtual machine migration are important technical details, but none of these presents a greater risk than a cloud provider going out of business.

Explain the Implications for Direct Cost and Cost Allocations

4. How does cloud adoption change financial management skills?
   A. Yearly budget cycles change because of rapid cloud elasticity.
   B. Cloud customers must monitor their own cloud resource usage and pay accordingly.
   C. OPEX becomes CAPEX.
   D. Cloud service costs are fixed.
   E. Performance monitoring should be performed by the cloud customer's IT staff.

   ☑ **A.** Instead of traditional yearly budget cycles, finance staff must account for the fact that rapid cloud elasticity will make OPEX variable.

   ☒ **B, C, D,** and **E** are incorrect. Cloud providers monitor customer usage, and they bill the customers accordingly, not the other way around. Cloud adoption changes CAPEX to OPEX, not the other way around. Even though cloud customer IT staff should be monitoring cloud service performance, this is not related to financial management skills.

5. Which of the following statements correctly reflects costs associated with cloud computing?
   A. There is an up-front capital investment.
   B. SLAs never contain cloud service termination fees.
   C. An organization's funds are used to acquire server hardware.
   D. Costs can be volatile.

   ☑ **D.** Cloud computing costs are generally volatile since cloud services can be provisioned and deprovisioned in a matter of minutes.

   ☒ **A, B,** and **C.** One benefit of cloud computing is that CAPEX becomes OPEX; therefore, there is no up-front capital investment as there would be if all IT services were hosted in-house. SLAs will normally contain clauses related to premature service termination fees. The cloud provider, not the cloud customer, acquires server hardware.

6. How can unpredictable costs associated with cloud services be managed? (Choose two.)
    A. Choose the cheapest cloud provider.
    B. Set limits on total costs for a given timeframe.
    C. Ensure costs are related to revenue.
    D. Prohibit IaaS from being used.

    ☑ **B** and **C.** Despite rapid elasticity, cloud costs can be managed by setting a limit on cloud-related costs and ensuring that these costs are relevant to the business.
    ☒ **A** and **D** are incorrect. Choosing the cheapest cloud provider is not a good strategy; there are many variables to consider besides cost. Even though prohibiting the use of IaaS could reduce cloud costs, **B** and **C** are better answers.

Understand How to Maintain Strategic Flexibility

7. What should you do to ensure your cloud data can be used with other cloud providers? (Choose two.)
    A. Use the fastest network connection possible.
    B. Know the format in which cloud data is stored.
    C. Know the maximum usable cloud storage capacity.
    D. Know the format cloud data can be exported to.

    ☑ **B** and **D.** Data stored in the cloud might be stored in its native file format and also might be exportable in its native format. For example, storing a Microsoft Excel spreadsheet file in the cloud might allow you to later export it as the same file. This means you could use the file without the cloud service provider, or you could upload this file to a different cloud service provider.
    ☒ **A** and **C** are related to cloud storage but have nothing to do with other cloud providers.

8. You are planning strategies related to your cloud provider becoming unavailable. Which of the following will ensure business continuity? (Choose two.)
    A. In-house hosting
    B. Cloud backup
    C. Network connectivity to the cloud provider
    D. Using an alternate cloud provider

☑   **A** and **D.** Should a cloud provider become unavailable, hosting IT services in-house or with other cloud providers are possible contingency plans that will ensure business continuity.

☒   **B** and **C** are incorrect. Cloud backup can ensure business continuity in the event of data loss but not if the cloud provider becomes unavailable. Network connectivity is always required to a cloud provider and is not relevant if the cloud provider is not reachable over the network.

A

About the
CD-ROM

T he CD-ROM included with this book comes complete with MasterExam software with practice exams and the electronic book in PDF format.

System Requirements

Software requires Windows XP Pro, Service Pack 2 or later, and Internet Explorer 8.0 or later, plus 200 MB of hard disk space for full installation. The electronic book requires Adobe Acrobat Reader.

Installing and Running MasterExam

If your computer CD-ROM drive is configured to auto run, the CD-ROM will automatically start up upon inserting the disk. From the opening screen you may install MasterExam by clicking the MasterExam link. This will begin the installation process and create a program group named LearnKey. To run MasterExam, use Start | All Programs | LearnKey | MasterExam. If the auto run feature did not launch your CD, browse to the CD and click on the LaunchTraining.exe icon. To register for the bonus MasterExam, simply click the Bonus MasterExam link on the main launch page and follow the directions to the free online registration.

MasterExam

MasterExam provides you with a simulation of the actual exam. The number of questions, the types of questions, and the time allowed are intended to be an accurate representation of the exam environment. You have the option to take an open-book exam, including hints, references, and answers; a closed-book exam; or the timed MasterExam simulation.

When you launch MasterExam, a digital clock display will appear in the bottom right-hand corner of your screen. The clock will continue to count down to zero unless you choose to end the exam before the time expires.

Help

A help file is provided through the Help button on the main page in the lower left-hand corner. An individual help feature is also available through MasterExam.

Removing Installation(s)

MasterExam is installed to your hard drive. For best results removing programs, use the Start | All Programs | LearnKey | Uninstall option to remove MasterExam.

Electronic Book

The entire contents of the book are provided in PDF format on the CD. This file is viewable on your computer and many portable devices. Adobe's Acrobat Reader is required to view the file on your PC and has been included on the CD. You may also use Adobe Digital Editions to access your electronic book.

For more information on Adobe Reader and to check for the most recent version of the software, visit Adobe's web site at www.adobe.com and search for the free Adobe Reader or look for Adobe Reader on the product page. Adobe Digital Editions can also be downloaded from the Adobe web site.

To view the electronic book on a portable device, copy the PDF file to your computer from the CD, and then copy the file to your portable device using a USB or other connection. Adobe does offer a mobile version of Adobe Reader, the Adobe Reader mobile app, which currently supports iOS and Android. For customers using Adobe Digital Editions and the iPad, you may have to download and install a separate reader program on your device. The Adobe web site has a list of recommended applications, and McGraw-Hill Education recommends the Bluefire Reader.

Technical Support

Technical Support information is provided in the following sections by feature.

LearnKey Technical Support

For technical problems with the software (installation, operation, removing installations), please visit www.learnkey.com, e-mail techsupport@learnkey.com, or call toll free 1-800-482-8244.

McGraw-Hill Content Support

For questions regarding the PDF copy of the book, e-mail techsolutions@mhedu.com or visit http://mhp.softwareassist.com.

For questions regarding book content, please e-mail customer.service@mheducation.com. For customers outside the United States, e-mail international_cs@mheducation.com.

B

Practice Exam

This practice exam is the same practice exam that is included on the CD-ROM that accompanies this book. It has been included for those readers who wish to practice in an alternative format.

Questions

1. Which of the following statements correctly explains the benefit of cloud computing?
   A. Cloud computing delivers a wide range of services.
   B. Cloud computing is procured by the IT department.
   C. Cloud computing delivers IT capacity on demand.
   D. Cloud computing delivers IT capabilities that scale with demand.

2. It is easy to exchange small text messages through Twitter. What is this an example of?
   A. IaaS
   B. PaaS
   C. SaaS
   D. None of the above

3. Which of the following statements best defines virtualization?
   A. Virtualization is a method to organize servers in a more efficient manner.
   B. Virtualization is a set of techniques for hiding software resources behind hardware abstractions.
   C. Virtualization is a method to structure data in a more efficient manner.
   D. Virtualization is a set of techniques for hiding hardware resources behind software abstractions.

4. When provisioning new virtual servers, which of the following must be done? (Choose two.)
   A. Specify cloud backup options for the virtual server.
   B. Specify the maximum server log file size.
   C. Specify user credentials to use with the virtual server.
   D. Specify the amount of RAM the virtual server will use.

5. Which definition applies to time-sharing?
   A. Individuals using computing resources at different times
   B. Individuals using computing resources simultaneously within isolated computing sessions
   C. Individuals using the same virtual servers simultaneously in the cloud
   D. Individuals using computing resources simultaneously within a shared computing session

6. Which of the following statements are true regarding cloud services? (Choose two.)
   A. Cloud services use a "pay-as-you-go" payment scheme.
   B. Cloud services are always less expensive than in-house hosted solutions.
   C. Cloud data storage is less secure than storing data locally.
   D. Cloud services can be provisioned quickly.

7. How can cloud computing improve the flexibility of businesses?
   A. Easier access by users outside of the organization
   B. Rapidly growing and shrinking capacity
   C. Faster deployment of applications
   D. All of the above
   E. None of the above

8. Cloud computing might not be beneficial for which of the following?
   A. Small engineering start-up
   B. Email system for the Pentagon
   C. Rapidly growing email system
   D. Web site of a large newspaper

9. Syl, a developer, is using cloud services to create and test a new application. What type of cloud service is Syl using?
   A. PaaS
   B. SaaS
   C. XaaS
   D. IaaS

10. Which of the following is not a typical business objective realized by IT outsourcing and cloud computing?
    A. Eliminating noncore activities
    B. Lack of skilled staff
    C. Improving cost structure
    D. Solving security problems

11. Which of the following statements is true?
    A. Cloud computing and outsourcing are the same.
    B. Outsourcing is specific to IT.
    C. Cloud computing is specific to IT.
    D. Outsourcing is cheaper than cloud computing.

12. Acme Incorporated is using a specific line-of-business piece of software and does not have the skilled help-desk staff required to support the software. What solution should Acme Incorporated employ?
    A. Migrate the application to the cloud.
    B. Virtualize the software.
    C. Host the software in-house.
    D. Outsource the help-desk staff requirement.

13. You are the IT administrator for a small regional airline that is opening a new office. To meet the airline's computing needs, you order server and desktop hardware, as well as the required software. Cloud computing can reduce or, in some cases, entirely eliminate these responsibilities from their customers. To which cloud characteristic does this scenario apply?
    A. Time to market
    B. Vendor lock-in
    C. Scalability
    D. Security

14. For a software development firm, which of the following cloud benefits is realized with PaaS?
    A. Time to market
    B. Vendor lock-in
    C. Scalability
    D. Security

15. How does cloud computing affect a cloud customer's cost structure?
    A. OPEX becomes CAPEX.
    B. CAPEX becomes OPEX.
    C. CAPEX increases.
    D. OPEX decreases.

16. With a cloud solution, which of the following IT tasks are the responsibility of the cloud provider? (Choose three.)
    A. Purchasing hardware
    B. Purchasing and licensing software
    C. Assigning user permissions to cloud data
    D. Updating software

17. Stacey, a financial analyst, is describing the business benefits of public cloud computing to her colleagues. Which of the following might she state? (Choose two.)

   A. Shorter time to market

   B. Decrease in operating expenses

   C. Facilitated data collaboration

   D. Increase in operating expenses

18. While _____ and _____ are important IT considerations to a business, they are not specific to cloud computing.

   A. backup, disaster recovery

   B. SLAs, SaaS

   C. virtualization, PaaS

   D. time to market, reduced CAPEX

19. Which statement regarding private clouds is true?

   A. SLAs are not required.

   B. Server virtualization is used only in public clouds.

   C. They are more secure than public clouds.

   D. They are for the exclusive use of a single organization.

20. Numerous cloud customers sharing the same computing services while having isolated computing environments is described as which of the following?

   A. Multitenancy

   B. Elasticity

   C. Virtualization

   D. XaaS

21. Which of the following are specific examples of IaaS? (Choose all that apply.)

   A. SLAs

   B. Software code libraries

   C. Cloud email accounts

   D. Cloud storage

22. Your organization uses on-premises servers to authenticate user logon requests. You would like to authorize user access to cloud email accounts using their local credentials. Which solution should you employ?

   A. Replicate local user accounts to the cloud.

   B. Use identity federation.

   C. Implement SaaS.

   D. Re-create user accounts in the cloud.

23. Relocating web content closer to users for quicker access is done using _____.
    A. content distribution networks
    B. identity federation
    C. virtualization
    D. cloud relocation

24. You are designing a solution to ensure your on-premises users will always have access to public cloud services. What should you consider?
    A. Identity federation
    B. Tablets instead of smartphones
    C. Redundant network connections
    D. Encryption

25. Cloud adoption does not remove the need for on-premises IT personnel. Which task must local IT personnel undertake to ensure cloud solutions are delivering business value?
    A. Setting limits on OPEX costs
    B. Monitoring application performance
    C. Creating new virtual machines
    D. Removing active virtual machines

26. Which of the following statements is true?
    A. PaaS is used to create web services.
    B. PaaS is used by end users.
    C. SaaS is used by software developers.
    D. Applications cannot be developed in the cloud.

27. What benefits are derived from PaaS?
    A. OPEX instead of CAPEX
    B. Cloud backup
    C. Rapid application development
    D. Elasticity

28. Which application should be migrated to the cloud for initial cloud testing?
    A. Financial management system
    B. Word processing
    C. Customer transaction database
    D. Emergency response system

29. Your company's application development team requires a self-provisioned software development solution that can quickly grow or shrink based on each project's parameters. Existing customer data will be used from a customized line-of-business application. What would you suggest?

A. Private PaaS

B. Private IaaS

C. Public PaaS

D. Public IaaS

30. Cloud solutions that can tolerate failures yet still provide service are referred to as what?

A. IaaS

B. Highly portable

C. PaaS

D. Highly available

31. You are evaluating cloud backup offerings from various cloud providers. What type of cloud service is cloud backup?

A. SaaS

B. IaaS

C. PaaS

D. DaaS

32. What is used to automate the provisioning of virtual machines?

A. SaaS

B. Management software

C. PaaS

D. Software libraries

33. Which of the following are risks associated with depending on cloud providers? (Choose two.)

A. Proprietary data formats

B. Lack of security

C. Vendor lock-in

D. User authentication

34. Which item usually presents a single point of failure in regard to cloud computing?

A. Network connection

B. Hard disk

C. Cloud backup

D. Virtual server

35. Which of the following statements regarding a change in IT roles as a result of cloud adoption is accurate?

    A. In-house IT personnel are no longer required.

    B. There will be an emphasis on managing operating expenses instead of capital expenses.

    C. There is no longer a need to back up business data.

    D. Private clouds could require IT personnel to provision services.

36. For in-house IT personnel, which IT task will be emphasized with cloud adoption?

    A. Application performance monitoring

    B. Security auditing

    C. Data backup

    D. High availability

37. What must be done to ensure the ongoing success of cloud service adoption?

    A. Software updates must be applied.

    B. Financial audits must take place.

    C. Industry compliance audits must take place.

    D. IT services must be coupled with specific business processes.

38. When evaluating cloud solutions, you conclude that some existing end-user software hosted on premises is not available as SaaS. What other options should you consider?

    A. Evaluate other functionally equivalent SaaS offerings.

    B. Keep using the on-premises end-user software.

    C. Use cloud backup for the end-user software data.

    D. Use PaaS instead.

39. Your company currently has six virtual servers hosted on premises using two clustered physical servers. The two physical servers on which the six virtual servers are running must be replaced. You have been asked to recommend the quickest solution to run the six virtual machines in the cloud instead of on the premises. What should you recommend?

    A. Back up the existing virtual servers. Create new cloud virtual servers and restore the data into them.

    B. Migrate the existing virtual machines to the cloud.

    C. You cannot migrate virtual machines to the cloud.

    D. Re-create the six virtual machines in the cloud from scratch.

40. Which of the following is a reason to migrate an application to the cloud?

    A. Elasticity.

    B. Data encryption.

    C. High availability.

    D. It will be cheaper than hosting the application in-house.

41. Which of the following items would show up in an SLA? (Choose all that apply.)

    A. Type of virtual server operating systems available

    B. PKI certificate for identity federation

    C. Degree of service elasticity

    D. Guaranteed level of service

42. Cloud adoption can increase the workload for cloud customer internal IT staff members in which way?

    A. Applying software patches

    B. Acquiring server hardware

    C. Monitoring cloud service performance

    D. Performing data backups

43. Planning disk capacity requirements in the cloud applies to which service management phase?

    A. Service Design

    B. Service Strategy

    C. Service Operation

    D. Service Transition

44. Encouraging cloud service use during minimal load times applies to which ITIL Service Strategy process?

    A. Capacity Management

    B. Demand Management

    C. Financial Management

    D. Service Level Management

45. Which process of the ITIL Service Design phase relates to ensuring cloud services are always accessible?

    A. Service Level Management

    B. Capacity Management

    C. Information Security Management

    D. Availability and Service Continuity Management

46. Choosing a cloud service that provides the same functionality as an in-house system applies to which ITIL life-cycle phase?

    A. Service Design

    B. Service Strategy

    C. Service Operation

    D. Service Transition

47. The manipulation of people to disclose confidential information defines what type of risk?

A. Malware

B. Denial of service

C. Password cracking

D. Social engineering

48. Why might a government agency be against storing its data in the cloud?

A. Clouds do not offer data encryption.

B. Data must be stored within national boundaries.

C. Data in virtual servers is unreliable.

D. Cloud data cannot be backed up.

49. What new IT service risk is a result of cloud adoption?

A. Loss of network connectivity

B. Loss of encryption keys

C. Loss of decryption keys

D. Failure of a hard disk

50. How does cloud adoption affect IT budgets?

A. IT budgets increase.

B. IT budgets decrease.

C. IT budgets remain the same.

D. IT budgets must account for the "pay-as-you-go" model.

Answers

1. Which of the following statements correctly explains the benefit of cloud computing?
   A. Cloud computing delivers a wide range of services.
   B. Cloud computing is procured by the IT department.
   C. Cloud computing delivers IT capacity on demand.
   D. Cloud computing delivers IT capabilities that scale with demand.

   ☑ **D.** Whether private or public cloud, IT services are delivered over a network and are quickly provisioned and deprovisioned as needed.

   ☒ **A, B,** and **C** are incorrect. Although there are many cloud offerings, stating that cloud computing delivers a wide range of services is too ambiguous. The IT department might provide support for or be consulted to evaluate cloud solutions, but the IT department would not procure the cloud solution. Computing infrastructure such as storage capacity can be increased in a cloud, but it is the IT capabilities (beyond just capacity) that make cloud solutions so compelling.

2. It is easy to exchange small text messages through Twitter. What is this an example of?
   A. IaaS
   B. PaaS
   C. SaaS
   D. None of the above

   ☑ **C.** Software as a Service is defined as productivity software, such as email or word processing or, in this case, Twitter, that is delivered over a network and available any time using any device.

   ☒ **A, B,** and **D** are incorrect. Infrastructure as a Service is rapidly scalable; it makes virtual servers, storage, backup, and similar computing infrastructure available over a network. Platform as a Service is used by developers; virtual machines, databases, and reusable software libraries make software development and testing quick and efficient.

3. Which of the following statements best defines virtualization?
   A. Virtualization is a method to organize servers in a more efficient manner.
   B. Virtualization is a set of techniques for hiding software resources behind hardware abstractions.
   C. Virtualization is a method to structure data in a more efficient manner.
   D. Virtualization is a set of techniques for hiding hardware resources behind software abstractions.

☑   **D.** Virtualization masks hardware resources so that each running virtual machine appears to have its own hardware.

☒   **A, B,** and **C** are incorrect. Organizing servers and data do not define the purpose of virtualization; they are both possible without virtualization. Virtualization hides hardware resources behind software abstractions, not the other way around.

4. When provisioning new virtual servers, which of the following must be done? (Choose two.)
   A. Specify cloud backup options for the virtual server.
   B. Specify the maximum server log file size.
   C. Specify user credentials to use with the virtual server.
   D. Specify the amount of RAM the virtual server will use.

☑   **C** and **D.** You must specify user credentials used with the new virtual server, and you must specify how much RAM the virtual machine will use.

☒   **A** and **B** are incorrect. Virtual servers do not have to use a cloud backup solution or any backup solution at all. The maximum server log file size is configured within the operating system and is not required when provisioning new virtual servers.

5. Which definition applies to time-sharing?
   A. Individuals using computing resources at different times
   B. Individuals using computing resources simultaneously within isolated computing sessions
   C. Individuals using the same virtual servers simultaneously in the cloud
   D. Individuals using computing resources simultaneously within a shared computing session

☑   **B.** Users could share expensive computing equipment at the same time by having their own isolated computing sessions.

☒   **A, C,** and **D** are incorrect. Time-sharing means people share computing hardware by having their own sessions at the same time. Virtual machines and shared user sessions are not related to this.

6. Which of the following statements are true regarding cloud services? (Choose two.)
   A. Cloud services use a "pay-as-you-go" payment scheme.
   B. Cloud services are always less expensive than in-house hosted solutions.
   C. Cloud data storage is less secure than storing data locally.
   D. Cloud services can be provisioned quickly.

☑ **A** and **D.** Instead of purchasing hardware and software, you purchase only the cloud IT solutions you use on an ongoing basis. Provisioning new cloud IT services, such as new virtual servers, is done very quickly compared to ordering physical server hardware and then installing an operating system on it.

☒ **B** and **C** are incorrect. Cloud solutions are not always less expensive than in-house solutions; this statement is too general. Security in the cloud is considered superior to that provided by a private organization. This is because cloud providers have the resources and expertise to exercise proper security controls, and they must pass third-party security audits often.

7. How can cloud computing improve the flexibility of businesses?
   A. Easier access by users outside of the organization
   B. Rapidly growing and shrinking capacity
   C. Faster deployment of applications
   D. All of the above
   E. None of the above

☑ **D.** Because public SaaS solutions are already on the Internet, any user who has been granted access can easily connect. Rapid elasticity allows businesses to respond to up and down swings in business activity, which in turn means businesses pay for the cloud services they use. PaaS allows developers to quickly create and test applications; this is made possible by software libraries and databases for developers and the rapid creation of virtual machines.

☒ **A, B, C,** and **E** are incorrect. Each listed item allows businesses to be flexible and to respond to changes in business volume.

8. Cloud computing might not be beneficial for which of the following?
   A. Small engineering start-up
   B. Email system for the Pentagon
   C. Rapidly growing email system
   D. Web site of a large newspaper

☑ **B.** Sensitive email systems, such as that used by the Pentagon, should be hosted in-house. This allows full control over the installation and use of the system.

☒ **A, C,** and **D** are incorrect. A small engineering start-up would benefit from not having to purchase server hardware, software, and licenses, as well as from not having to hire the expertise to configure the system. Any IT need for rapid scalability is served well by cloud computing, such as a rapidly growing email system. Newspaper web sites can benefit since ensuring the availability of the web site can be detailed in an SLA.

9. Syl, a developer, is using cloud services to create and test a new application. What type of cloud service is Syl using?

A. PaaS

B. SaaS

C. XaaS

D. IaaS

   ☑ **A.** PaaS allows developers to quickly create and test applications.

   ☒ **B, C,** and **D** are incorrect. SaaS allows end users to access software over a network any time, from any device. XaaS is an all-encompassing term that refers to any IT service delivered over a network. IaaS offers computing infrastructure such as virtual servers, network, and storage to cloud consumers over a network.

10. Which of the following is not a typical business objective realized by IT outsourcing and cloud computing?

A. Eliminating noncore activities

B. Lack of skilled staff

C. Improving cost structure

D. Solving security problems

   ☑ **D.** Security problems are not a typical reason for outsourcing or cloud adoption.

   ☒ **A, B,** and **C** are incorrect. Eliminating noncore activities, a lack of internal skilled staff, and improving cost structure (CAPEX to OPEX) are all common reasons that companies choose to outsource or adopt cloud solutions. Remember that cloud computing is a form of outsourcing.

11. Which of the following statements is true?

A. Cloud computing and outsourcing are the same.

B. Outsourcing is specific to IT.

C. Cloud computing is specific to IT.

D. Outsourcing is cheaper than cloud computing.

   ☑ **C.** Cloud computing is essentially IT outsourcing, at least from a business perspective.

   ☒ **A, B,** and **D** are incorrect. Cloud computing is specific to IT, and outsourcing is not; thus, they are not exactly the same. Outsourcing cannot be compared to cloud computing in terms of always being cheaper because cloud computing is specific to IT; outsourcing could be related to any kind of skilled work.

12. Acme Incorporated is using a specific line-of-business piece of software and does not have the skilled help-desk staff required to support the software. What solution should Acme Incorporated employ?

    A. Migrate the application to the cloud.

    B. Virtualize the software.

    C. Host the software in-house.

    D. Outsource the help-desk staff requirement.

    ☑ **D.** Acme Incorporated needs skilled help-desk staff to support its specific software. Outsourcing is usually the result of a lack of specific skill sets within an organization.

    ☒ **A, B,** and **C** are incorrect. Migrating the application to the cloud, virtualizing the line-of-business software, and hosting it in-house do not address the core problem, which is a lack of skilled help-desk staff.

13. You are the IT administrator for a small regional airline that is opening a new office. To meet the airline's computing needs, you order server and desktop hardware, as well as the required software. Cloud computing can reduce or, in some cases, entirely eliminate these responsibilities from their customers. To which cloud characteristic does this scenario apply?

    A. Time to market

    B. Vendor lock-in

    C. Scalability

    D. Security

    ☑ **C.** Scalability embodies the ability to grow in a controlled manner, as in increasing computing infrastructure as business needs demand.

    ☒ **A, B,** and **D** are incorrect. A reduction in time to market for new products and services gives a company a competitive edge, but it does not apply to the scenario. Vendor lock-in ties customers to vendor-specific solutions, which is not the case here. Security does apply to cloud computing, but it does not relate to this scenario, where new hardware and software must be procured.

14. For a software development firm, which of the following cloud benefits is realized with PaaS?

    A. Time to market

    B. Vendor lock-in

    C. Scalability

    D. Security

☑ **A.** PaaS allows developers to quickly create and test applications. Getting your product to market before your competitors can give a competitive edge.

☒ **B, C,** and **D** are incorrect. Vendor lock-in ties customers to vendor-specific solutions, but this is not a benefit of PaaS. Scalability embodies the ability to grow in a controlled manner, but it is not a distinguishing feature of PaaS as compared to other types of cloud offerings. Security does apply to cloud computing but not specifically to PaaS.

15. How does cloud computing affect a cloud customer's cost structure?
    A. OPEX becomes CAPEX.
    B. CAPEX becomes OPEX.
    C. CAPEX increases.
    D. OPEX decreases.

☑ **B.** Instead of spending capital to acquire computing hardware, software, and licenses, cloud customers can essentially rent the IT services they need as they need them; thus, capital expenditures (CAPEX) become operating expenses (OPEX).

☒ **A, C,** and **D** are incorrect. OPEX does not become CAPEX with cloud adoption; CAPEX becomes OPEX. CAPEX decreases with cloud adoption, and OPEX increases.

16. With a cloud solution, which of the following IT tasks are the responsibility of the cloud provider? (Choose three.)
    A. Purchasing hardware
    B. Purchasing and licensing software
    C. Assigning user permissions to cloud data
    D. Updating software

☑ **A, B,** and **D.** Cloud providers are responsible for all aspects of hardware and software for their cloud solutions.

☒ **C** is incorrect. The cloud customer assigns user permissions to cloud data.

17. Stacey, a financial analyst, is describing the business benefits of public cloud computing to her colleagues. Which of the following might she state? (Choose two.)
    A. Shorter time to market
    B. Decrease in operating expenses
    C. Facilitated data collaboration
    D. Increase in operating expenses

☑ **A and C.** Cloud solutions remove the need to wait for physical computing hardware to arrive as IT needs grow, and provisioning of IT services is done very quickly thanks to virtualization; these factors reduce the amount of time a business takes to get a product or service to their customers. Data stored in the cloud is easily accessible from anywhere and thus facilitates data collaboration.

☒ **B and D** are incorrect. Cloud computing increases operating expenses because of ongoing subscription and usage fees, while capital expenditures decrease. An increase in any type of cost is never a benefit to the payer.

18. While _____ and _____ are important IT considerations to a business, they are not specific to cloud computing.
   A. backup, disaster recovery
   B. SLAs, SaaS
   C. virtualization, PaaS
   D. time to market, reduced CAPEX

☑ **A.** Backup and disaster recovery are critically important to any business using any type of IT solution, not just cloud customers.

☒ **B, C,** and **D** are incorrect. SaaS and PaaS are specific to cloud computing. Time to market and CAPEX are not IT considerations; they are business strategy and financial considerations.

19. Which statement regarding private clouds is true?
   A. SLAs are not required.
   B. Server virtualization is used only in public clouds.
   C. They are more secure than public clouds.
   D. They are for the exclusive use of a single organization.

☑ **D.** Private clouds use computing assets owned by, and for the exclusive use by, a single organization.

☒ **A, B,** and **C** are incorrect. Private clouds still use SLAs to guarantee levels of service to business units. The use of server virtualization is not exclusive to public clouds. Public cloud providers generally have more resources, have more expertise, and must pass frequent third-party audits. This suggests public cloud providers must exercise the strictest security standards.

20. Numerous cloud customers sharing the same computing services while having isolated computing environments is described as which of the following?
    A. Multitenancy
    B. Elasticity
    C. Virtualization
    D. XaaS

    ☑ **A.** Multitenancy allows multiple cloud customers to use the same computing services such as cloud mailboxes, but the cloud provider ensures each cloud customer is kept isolated from another.
    ☒ **B, C,** and **D** are incorrect. Elasticity refers to the ease with which cloud services can grow or shrink to meet business demand. Virtualization allows multiple operating systems to run simultaneously on a single computing device. XaaS is a catchall term referring to any computing service delivered over a network.

21. Which of the following are specific examples of IaaS? (Choose all that apply.)
    A. SLAs
    B. Software code libraries
    C. Cloud email accounts
    D. Cloud storage

    ☑ **D.** IaaS provides computing infrastructure services such as virtual servers, virtual networks, cloud backup, and cloud storage.
    ☒ **A, B,** and **C** are incorrect. SLAs describe levels of service that will be provided to a customer, but they are not specific to IaaS. Software code libraries are of use to software developers; this is PaaS, not IaaS. Cloud email accounts are an example of SaaS, not IaaS.

22. Your organization uses on-premises servers to authenticate user logon requests. You would like to authorize user access to cloud email accounts using their local credentials. Which solution should you employ?
    A. Replicate local user accounts to the cloud.
    B. Use identity federation.
    C. Implement SaaS.
    D. Re-create user accounts in the cloud.

☑ **B.** Identity federation uses a single identity provider to authorize user access to multiple software applications, including cloud apps.

☒ **A, C,** and **D** are incorrect. Replicating user accounts to the cloud means you are not using the on-premises user identities, which is required in this scenario. SaaS provides end-user software services over a network and has nothing to do with authentication or authorization. Re-creating user accounts in the cloud is unacceptable; the scenario clearly states that local user accounts are to be used for authentication.

23. Relocating web content closer to users for quicker access is done using _____.
   A. content distribution networks
   B. identity federation
   C. virtualization
   D. cloud relocation

☑ **A.** Content distribution networks place cloud content closer physically to users, which enhances the user experience because of quicker access.

☒ **B, C,** and **D** are incorrect. Identity federation uses a single identity provider to authorize access to numerous computing services. Virtualization makes cloud solutions possible, but it does not place content closer to users. Cloud relocation is a fictitious term.

24. You are designing a solution to ensure your on-premises users will always have access to public cloud services. What should you consider?
   A. Identity federation
   B. Tablets instead of smartphones
   C. Redundant network connections
   D. Encryption

☑ **C.** A single network connection to a cloud provider presents a single point of failure.

☒ **A, B,** and **D** are incorrect. Identity federation uses a single identity provider to authorize access to numerous computing services; it does not ensure access to cloud services. Whether users use tablets, laptops, smartphones, or desktops does not affect whether cloud services are reachable. Encryption protects sensitive data from unauthorized use but is not related to accessing cloud services.

25. Cloud adoption does not remove the need for on-premises IT personnel. Which task must local IT personnel undertake to ensure cloud solutions are delivering business value?

A. Setting limits on OPEX costs

B. Monitoring application performance

C. Creating new virtual machines

D. Removing active virtual machines

☑ **B.** Local IT personnel must monitor cloud solutions to ensure optimal performance. Underperforming cloud solutions could be because of sluggish network connections or overburdened cloud providers, and this reduces the value offered by cloud computing.

☒ **A, C,** and **D** are incorrect. Setting limits on OPEX is not the responsibility of the IT staff. The creation of virtual machines can be important with cloud solutions but not as important to business value as optimal performance. Removing inactive virtual machines can benefit the business because of less cost, but removing active virtual machines cannot.

26. Which of the following statements is true?

A. PaaS is used to create web services.

B. PaaS is used by end users.

C. SaaS is used by software developers.

D. Applications cannot be developed in the cloud.

☑ **A.** PaaS is used by software developers to create and test applications. These applications typically take the form of web services.

☒ **B, C,** and **D** are incorrect. PaaS is used by software developers, not end users. SaaS is used by end users, not software developers. Applications can be developed and tested in the cloud; this is precisely what PaaS is for.

27. What benefits are derived from PaaS?

A. OPEX instead of CAPEX

B. Cloud backup

C. Rapid application development

D. Elasticity

☑ **C.** PaaS provides reusable software libraries, databases, virtual machines, storage, and so on, to software developers to decrease the amount of time it takes to create and test software applications.

☒ **A, B,** and **D** are incorrect. Shifting CAPEX to OPEX is a benefit of all cloud models, not just PaaS. Cloud backup falls under IaaS, not PaaS. Elasticity is a benefit of all cloud models, not just PaaS.

28. Which application should be migrated to the cloud for initial cloud testing?
   A. Financial management system
   B. Word processing
   C. Customer transaction database
   D. Emergency response system

☑ **B.** Noncritical software such as a word processor should be tested first in the cloud.

☒ **A, C,** and **D** are incorrect. Sensitive or mission-critical software related to finances, customer transactions, or emergency response are not good cloud pilot choices; less critical software would be a wiser choice.

29. Your company's application development team requires a self-provisioned software development solution that can quickly grow or shrink based on each project's parameters. Existing customer data will be used from a customized line-of-business application. What would you suggest?
   A. Private PaaS
   B. Private IaaS
   C. Public PaaS
   D. Public IaaS

☑ **A.** Since customer data stored in a customized line-of-business app is needed, private PaaS makes the most sense.

☒ **B, C,** and **D** are incorrect. Private and public IaaS do not apply to developing software applications in a cloud environment; IaaS provides computing infrastructure such as cloud storage. Getting data from a customized app into a public cloud could prove to be complex.

30. Cloud solutions that can tolerate failures yet still provide service are referred to as what?
   A. IaaS
   B. Highly portable
   C. PaaS
   D. Highly available

☑ **D.** High availability ensures cloud solutions are always accessible. This means eliminating single points of failure such as storing data on a single hard disk or single network connections.

☒ **A, B,** and **C** are incorrect. IaaS offers computing infrastructure services over the cloud, and PaaS offers software development capabilities over the cloud; by themselves neither tolerates failures. Highly portable means something can be moved from one system to another with ease; this is not related to high availability.

31. You are evaluating cloud backup offerings from various cloud providers. What type of cloud service is cloud backup?
    A. SaaS
    B. IaaS
    C. PaaS
    D. DaaS

☑ **B.** IaaS cloud service offerings include virtual servers, cloud storage, cloud backup, virtual networks, and so on.

☒ **A, C,** and **D** are incorrect. SaaS offers end-user software over a network. PaaS allows developers to easily and quickly create and test applications. DaaS makes remote virtual desktops available to users from any device; the processing occurs on the desktop virtualization server.

32. What is used to automate the provisioning of virtual machines?
    A. SaaS
    B. Management software
    C. PaaS
    D. Software libraries

☑ **B.** Cloud providers have management software, usually web-based, that is used to automate virtual machine provisioning.

☒ **A, C,** and **D** are incorrect. SaaS offers end-user software over a network. PaaS allows developers to easily and quickly create and test applications. Software libraries are made available to developers with PaaS offerings.

33. Which of the following are risks associated with depending on cloud providers? (Choose two.)
    A. Proprietary data formats
    B. Lack of security
    C. Vendor lock-in
    D. User authentication

☑ **A** and **C.** If cloud data is stored in a proprietary format and you decide to have that data hosted in-house or you decide to switch cloud providers, your data will be inaccessible. Vendor lock-in occurs when cloud customers are stuck with using a specific cloud provider's management tools.

☒ **B** and **D** are incorrect. There is no further security risk with cloud solutions than there otherwise would be. User authentication is not a risk; it is required for users to be authorized to various cloud services.

34. Which item usually presents a single point of failure in regard to cloud computing?

    A. Network connection

    B. Hard disk

    C. Cloud backup

    D. Virtual server

☑ **A.** Because cloud services are accessible over a network, it is important to have redundant network links.

☒ **B, C,** and **D** are incorrect. Cloud providers always ensure that hard disks used for cloud storage and backup, as well as virtual server files, are on-disk arrays that are mirrored. In addition, all of this data might be replicated to another data center run by the cloud provider.

35. Which of the following statements regarding a change in IT roles as a result of cloud adoption is accurate?

    A. In-house IT personnel are no longer required.

    B. There will be an emphasis on managing operating expenses instead of capital expenses.

    C. There is no longer a need to back up business data.

    D. Private clouds could require IT personnel to provision services.

☑ **D.** Provisioning services, and not servers, will be a skill that IT staff members must possess.

☒ **A, B,** and **C** are incorrect. In-house IT personnel are required to maintain adequate cloud computing client devices, to maintain network connections to cloud providers, to provision cloud services, and to evaluate new innovative cloud solutions. IT is not responsible for financial management. Cloud solutions still require an appropriate backup strategy.

36. For in-house IT personnel, which IT task will be emphasized with cloud adoption?
- A. Application performance monitoring
- B. Security auditing
- C. Data backup
- D. High availability

> ☑ **A.** Monitoring the performance and availability of cloud services, and the network connection to them, is an important skill resulting from cloud adoption.
> ☒ **B, C,** and **D** are incorrect. Security auditing, data backup, and high availability are the concern of the cloud provider, not the cloud customer.

37. What must be done to ensure the ongoing success of cloud service adoption?
- A. Software updates must be applied.
- B. Financial audits must take place.
- C. Industry compliance audits must take place.
- D. IT services must be coupled with specific business processes.

> ☑ **D.** To provide business value, all IT services must serve the needs of the business.
> ☒ **A, B,** and **C** are incorrect. Cloud providers are responsible for applying software updates for cloud services. Financial and industry compliance audits are always relevant; however, this should be considered before cloud adoption, not after.

38. When evaluating cloud solutions, you conclude that some existing end-user software hosted on premises is not available as SaaS. What other options should you consider?
- A. Evaluate other functionally equivalent SaaS offerings.
- B. Keep using the on-premises end-user software.
- C. Use cloud backup for the end-user software data.
- D. Use PaaS instead.

> ☑ **A.** Cloud providers might have a SaaS offering that has the same functionality of the in-house software in use. This should be explored first.
> ☒ **B, C,** and **D** are incorrect. Since cloud evaluation was part of the question, keeping the existing software solution is not the best choice. Cloud backup does not address the issue of using a cloud SaaS solution. PaaS is for developers to quickly create and test applications, not end-user productivity software.

39. Your company currently has six virtual servers hosted on premises using two clustered physical servers. The two physical servers on which the six virtual servers are running must be replaced. You have been asked to recommend the quickest solution to run the six virtual machines in the cloud instead of on the premises. What should you recommend?

   A. Back up the existing virtual servers. Create new cloud virtual servers and restore the data into them.
   B. Migrate the existing virtual machines to the cloud.
   C. You cannot migrate virtual machines to the cloud.
   D. Re-create the six virtual machines in the cloud from scratch.

   ☑ **B.** Migrating existing virtual machines to the cloud is the quickest solution. Most cloud providers offer this solution.
   ☒ **A, C,** and **D** are incorrect. Creating new virtual servers in the cloud and restoring data to them normally takes longer than simply migrating virtual servers to the cloud. Most cloud providers offering IaaS allow cloud customers to migrate virtual machines to the cloud.

40. Which of the following is a reason to migrate an application to the cloud?

   A. Elasticity.
   B. Data encryption.
   C. High availability.
   D. It will be cheaper than hosting the application in-house.

   ☑ **A.** Cloud elasticity means the application can grow or shrink relative to business needs.
   ☒ **B, C,** and **D** are incorrect. Data encryption and high availability are available without migrating an application to the cloud. Even though CAPEX gets shifted to OPEX, when viewed over time, cloud solutions are not always cheaper than in-house solutions.

41. Which of the following items would show up in an SLA? (Choose all that apply.)

   A. Type of virtual server operating systems available
   B. PKI certificate for identity federation
   C. Degree of service elasticity
   D. Guaranteed level of service

   ☑ **C** and **D.** Service elasticity, that is, the ability to increase or decrease a cloud service such as the number of user mailboxes, should be stated in the SLA. All SLAs state the expected level of service cloud customers can expect and the repercussions if those service levels are not met.
   ☒ **A** and **B** are incorrect. The type of operating system used in virtual machines, along with PKI certificate details, are not relevant to the SLA, even though they might be of technical relevance.

42. Cloud adoption can increase the workload for cloud customer internal IT staff members in which way?
   A.   Applying software patches
   B.   Acquiring server hardware
   C.   Monitoring cloud service performance
   D.   Performing data backups

   ☑   **C.** With cloud adoption, IT staff members will find themselves focusing more on the delivery, monitoring, and maintenance of IT services.
   ☒   **A, B,** and **D** are incorrect. Applying software patches, acquiring server hardware, and performing backups are tasks performed by the cloud provider.

43. Planning disk capacity requirements in the cloud applies to which service management phase?
   A.   Service Design
   B.   Service Strategy
   C.   Service Operation
   D.   Service Transition

   ☑   **A.** Capacity planning falls under the Service Design phase.
   ☒   **B, C,** and **D** are incorrect. Capacity planning, such as cloud storage, does not apply to these ITIL life-cycle phases.

44. Encouraging cloud service use during minimal load times applies to which ITIL Service Strategy process?
   A.   Capacity Management
   B.   Demand Management
   C.   Financial Management
   D.   Service Level Management

   ☑   **B.** Demand Management ensures customer capacity demands can be met. Discouraging IT service use during peak busy times falls into this description.
   ☒   **A, C,** and **D** are incorrect. These ITIL processes do not map directly to encouraging the use of IT services during less busy times like Demand Management does.

45. Which process of the ITIL Service Design phase relates to ensuring cloud services are always accessible?

A. Service Level Management
B. Capacity Management
C. Information Security Management
D. Availability and Service Continuity Management

☑ **D.** Availability and Service Continuity Management ensures that IT services are always accessible by managing risks that could impact IT service delivery.

☒ **A, B,** and **C** are incorrect. Service Level Management relates to ensuring that SLA terms map to business requirements. Capacity Management ensures IT service capacity can be met in line with SLA terms. Information Security Management allows only authorized users to access any IT-related service or data belonging to an organization.

46. Choosing a cloud service that provides the same functionality as an in-house system applies to which ITIL life-cycle phase?

A. Service Design
B. Service Strategy
C. Service Operation
D. Service Transition

☑ **A.** Evaluating functional equivalents of in-house IT systems relates to the Service Design phase.

☒ **B, C,** and **D** are incorrect. Service Strategy involves defining and implementing service strategies. Service Operation focuses on making sure IT services are accessible and available at all times in the most efficient and cost-effective way possible. Service Transition relates to processes such as Change Management, Configuration Management, and Asset Management.

47. The manipulation of people to disclose confidential information defines what type of risk?

A. Malware
B. Denial of service
C. Password cracking
D. Social engineering

☑ **D.** Tricking people to disclose sensitive information is referred to as social engineering. This could be as simple as an imposter posing as a help-desk member calling an end user and asking for password information.

☒ **A, B,** and **C** are incorrect. Malware is software that performs malicious actions, such as deleting files from a hard disk. Denial-of-service attacks render a network service unusable to legitimate users. Password cracking involves breaking into user accounts once the password has been determined, usually by automated means.

48. Why might a government agency be against storing its data in the cloud?
    A. Clouds do not offer data encryption.
    B. Data must be stored within national boundaries.
    C. Data in virtual servers is unreliable.
    D. Cloud data cannot be backed up.

☑ **B.** Some cloud providers have data centers in many countries, and data from one country might be replicated to another; this could present legal and jurisdiction ambiguities.

☒ **A, C,** and **D** are incorrect. Many cloud solutions offer encryption, and for those that do not, you can encrypt your data before storing it in the cloud. Virtual servers are very reliable, and so is their data. Cloud data can be backed up.

49. What new IT service risk is a result of cloud adoption?
    A. Loss of network connectivity
    B. Loss of encryption keys
    C. Loss of decryption keys
    D. Failure of a hard disk

☑ **A.** Losing network connectivity means losing access to cloud IT services and data. Redundant network connections should be configured.

☒ **B, C,** and **D** are incorrect. Encryption and decryption key loss is not a problem specific to cloud adoption. Cloud providers use redundant disk arrays for data, so a hard disk failure will not interrupt IT service operation.

50. How does cloud adoption affect IT budgets?

   A. IT budgets increase.
   B. IT budgets decrease.
   C. IT budgets remain the same.
   D. IT budgets must account for the "pay-as-you-go" model.

☑   **D.** Instead of a yearly or quarterly IT budget cycle, cloud elasticity means costs are much more variable.

☒   **A, B,** and **C** are incorrect. IT budgets normally decrease to reflect the lack of capital expenditures. This may take time to become apparent because of asset depreciation methods of accounting, as well as ongoing OPEX.

Glossary

Anything as a Service (XaaS)   This refers to any IT service delivered over a network.

application programming interface (API)   An API is a collection of software routines used to interact with a software component.

application service provider (ASP)   An ASP is an entity offering hosted applications.

asynchronous JavaScript and XML (Ajax)   Ajax is a web development technique allowing partial web page updating.

bandwidth   This is the amount of data, over a period of time (normally seconds), that can be transmitted between two points.

CAPEX   This stands for capital expenditure.

cloud bursting   This means using public cloud services (beyond private cloud resources) during peak business times.

cloud computing   Cloud computing consists of pooled computing resources offered by a provider to customers over a network as a "pay-as-you-go" model.

cloud elasticity   This is the ability to quickly provision and deprovision IT services.

cloud exit strategy   This is a contingency plan used if a cloud provider is no longer available or is the plan used to discontinue a relationship with a provider regardless of the underlying reason.

cloud fabric   This is the computing infrastructure used for a public or private cloud.

comma-separated value (CSV)   CSV is a standard format for data exchange between dissimilar systems.

community cloud   This is a multitenant computing environment delivering IT services to organizations that have similar IT computing and security needs.

configuration item (CI)   A CI is an IT resource that is tracked in a CMDB.

configuration management database (CMDB)   A CMDB is a repository of information about IT components related to IT processes, services, and the value they represent.

content distribution network (CDN)   A CDN is a collection of servers that are used to provide web content to users in the quickest possible manner by placing that content near the user.

data confidentiality   This means encrypting data so that only authorized parties are granted access.

data integrity   This means ensuring that data has not been tampered with or damaged and that it comes from a trusted source.

Extensible Markup Language (XML)   XML is a standard format that uses data descriptor tags to express data.

hybrid cloud   This is a combination of private and public cloud services.

HyperText Transfer Protocol Secure (HTTPS)   HTTPS is a web protocol used between web browsers and web servers to securely transmit data.

identity federation   This is the use of a single identity provider to authorize users to multiple web applications without the user authenticating to each web application.

Information Technology Infrastructure Library (ITIL)   ITIL consists of recommended methods to ensure that IT services align with business needs. ITIL is a framework of processes.

Infrastructure as a Service (IaaS)   This type of cloud provider uses a third party to provide server, storage, and other IT capabilities over a network.

JavaScript Object Notation (JSON)   JSON is a variation of the JavaScript scripting language designed for data exchange.

multitenancy   This is when multiple cloud customers share a pool of computing resources made available by a cloud provider.

network latency   This is the delay of data transmission between two endpoints.

OPEX   This stands for operating expense.

Payment Card Industry Data Security Standard (PCI DSS)   PCI DSS is a set of standards that companies involved with debit and credit card transactions must meet.

Platform as a Service (PaaS)   This type of cloud provider makes computing resources such as virtual servers, databases, storage, and software development libraries available to developers.

private cloud   Private clouds consist of self-provisioned and elastic computing services offered for the exclusive use of an organization using an organization's computing assets.

public cloud   Public clouds consist of self-provisioned and elastic computing services offered to the general public over the Internet.

Public Key Infrastructure (PKI)   PKI is a hierarchy of digital security certificates issued to users or computers for the purposes of authentication and data security.

relying party   In a federated environment, this is the party that relies on security claims authenticated by an identity provider.

rich Internet application (RIA)   An RIA is a web application with an extensive feature set rivaling that of traditional desktop software.

risk management   This is an analysis of items that have a potential negative impact on an organization and the possible mitigating strategies.

Sarbanes-Oxley Act (SOA)   The SOA is a set of American laws whereby organizations must prove they have control of their assets in order to verify the accuracy of financial records.

Secure Sockets Layer (SSL)   SSL is a security protocol that protects network transmissions using encryption and digital signatures.

Security Assertion Markup Language (SAML)   SAML is an XML method of exchanging user or computer authentication and authorization messages between identity providers and relying parties.

service level agreement (SLA)   An SLA is a contractual document stipulating the terms surrounding cloud provider services, including the termination of cloud services.

single sign-on (SSO)   SSO passes authentication information from a single authentication sequence to computing services that would each normally require their own separate authentication.

social engineering   This is the manipulation of people to disclose confidential information.

Software as a Service (SaaS)   This type of provider makes application software available over a network any time, from any place, using any device.

storage area network (SAN)   A SAN is a communication network dedicated to transmitting disk input and output traffic.

time-sharing   This is when multiple users consume computing resources at the same time on the same system using independent computing sessions.

vendor lock-in   This is when there is dependency on a specific provider solution.

virtual private network (VPN)   A VPN is an encrypted network connection between two devices over an untrusted network, allowing access to network resources on an endpoint network.

virtualization   This is a means of masking physical hardware resources such as computers, storage, and networking to software operating systems running in virtual machines.

INDEX

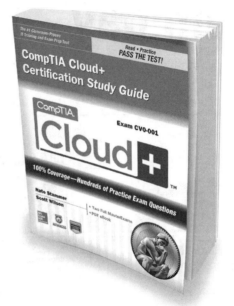

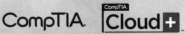

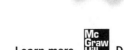

LICENSE AGREEMENT

THIS PRODUCT (THE "PRODUCT") CONTAINS PROPRIETARY SOFTWARE, DATA AND INFORMATION (INCLUDING DOCUMENTATION) OWNED BY McGRAW-HILL EDUCATION AND ITS LICENSORS. YOUR RIGHT TO USE THE PRODUCT IS GOVERNED BY THE TERMS AND CONDITIONS OF THIS AGREEMENT.

LICENSE: Throughout this License Agreement, "you" shall mean either the individual or the entity whose agent opens this package. You are granted a non-exclusive and non-transferable license to use the Product subject to the following terms:

(i) If you have licensed a single user version of the Product, the Product may only be used on a single computer (i.e., a single CPU). If you licensed and paid the fee applicable to a local area network or wide area network version of the Product, you are subject to the terms of the following subparagraph (ii).

(ii) If you have licensed a local area network version, you may use the Product on unlimited workstations located in one single building selected by you that is served by such local area network. If you have licensed a wide area network version, you may use the Product on unlimited workstations located in multiple buildings on the same site selected by you that is served by such wide area network; provided, however, that any building will not be considered located in the same site if it is more than five (5) miles away from any building included in such site. In addition, you may only use a local area or wide area network version of the Product on one single server. If you wish to use the Product on more than one server, you must obtain written authorization from McGraw-Hill Education and pay additional fees.

(iii) You may make one copy of the Product for back-up purposes only and you must maintain an accurate record as to the location of the back-up at all times.

COPYRIGHT; RESTRICTIONS ON USE AND TRANSFER: All rights (including copyright) in and to the Product are owned by McGraw-Hill Education and its licensors. You are the owner of the enclosed disc on which the Product is recorded. You may not use, copy, decompile, disassemble, reverse engineer, modify, reproduce, create derivative works, transmit, distribute, sublicense, store in a database or retrieval system of any kind, rent or transfer the Product, or any portion thereof, in any form or by any means (including electronically or otherwise) except as expressly provided for in this License Agreement. You must reproduce the copyright notices, trademark notices, legends and logos of McGraw-Hill Education and its licensors that appear on the Product on the back-up copy of the Product which you are permitted to make hereunder. All rights in the Product not expressly granted herein are reserved by McGraw-Hill Education and its licensors.

TERM: This License Agreement is effective until terminated. It will terminate if you fail to comply with any term or condition of this License Agreement. Upon termination, you are obligated to return to McGraw-Hill Education the Product together with all copies thereof and to purge all copies of the Product included in any and all servers and computer facilities.

DISCLAIMER OF WARRANTY: THE PRODUCT AND THE BACK-UP COPY ARE LICENSED "AS IS." McGRAW-HILL EDUCATION, ITS LICENSORS AND THE AUTHORS MAKE NO WARRANTIES, EXPRESS OR IMPLIED, AS TO THE RESULTS TO BE OBTAINED BY ANY PERSON OR ENTITY FROM USE OF THE PRODUCT, ANY INFORMATION OR DATA INCLUDED THEREIN AND/OR ANY TECHNICAL SUPPORT SERVICES PROVIDED HEREUNDER, IF ANY ("TECHNICAL SUPPORT SERVICES"). McGRAW-HILL EDUCATION, ITS LICENSORS AND THE AUTHORS MAKE NO EXPRESS OR IMPLIED WARRANTIES OF MERCHANTABILITY OR FITNESS FOR A PARTICULAR PURPOSE OR USE WITH RESPECT TO THE PRODUCT. McGRAW-HILL EDUCATION, ITS LICENSORS, AND THE AUTHORS MAKE NO GUARANTEE THAT YOU WILL PASS ANY CERTIFICATION EXAM WHATSOEVER BY USING THIS PRODUCT. NEITHER McGRAW-HILL EDUCATION, ANY OF ITS LICENSORS NOR THE AUTHORS WARRANT THAT THE FUNCTIONS CONTAINED IN THE PRODUCT WILL MEET YOUR REQUIREMENTS OR THAT THE OPERATION OF THE PRODUCT WILL BE UNINTERRUPTED OR ERROR FREE. YOU ASSUME THE ENTIRE RISK WITH RESPECT TO THE QUALITY AND PERFORMANCE OF THE PRODUCT.

LIMITED WARRANTY FOR DISC: To the original licensee only, McGraw-Hill Education warrants that the enclosed disc on which the Product is recorded is free from defects in materials and workmanship under normal use and service for a period of ninety (90) days from the date of purchase. In the event of a defect in the disc covered by the foregoing warranty, McGraw-Hill Education will replace the disc.

LIMITATION OF LIABILITY: NEITHER McGRAW-HILL EDUCATION, ITS LICENSORS NOR THE AUTHORS SHALL BE LIABLE FOR ANY INDIRECT, SPECIAL OR CONSEQUENTIAL DAMAGES, SUCH AS BUT NOT LIMITED TO, LOSS OF ANTICIPATED PROFITS OR BENEFITS, RESULTING FROM THE USE OR INABILITY TO USE THE PRODUCT EVEN IF ANY OF THEM HAS BEEN ADVISED OF THE POSSIBILITY OF SUCH DAMAGES. THIS LIMITATION OF LIABILITY SHALL APPLY TO ANY CLAIM OR CAUSE WHATSOEVER WHETHER SUCH CLAIM OR CAUSE ARISES IN CONTRACT, TORT, OR OTHERWISE. Some states do not allow the exclusion or limitation of indirect, special or consequential damages, so the above limitation may not apply to you.

U.S. GOVERNMENT RESTRICTED RIGHTS: Any software included in the Product is provided with restricted rights subject to subparagraphs (c), (1) and (2) of the Commercial Computer Software-Restricted Rights clause at 48 C.F.R. 52.227-19. The terms of this Agreement applicable to the use of the data in the Product are those under which the data are generally made available to the general public by McGraw-Hill Education. Except as provided herein, no reproduction, use, or disclosure rights are granted with respect to the data included in the Product and no right to modify or create derivative works from any such data is hereby granted.

GENERAL: This License Agreement constitutes the entire agreement between the parties relating to the Product. The terms of any Purchase Order shall have no effect on the terms of this License Agreement. Failure of McGraw-Hill Education to insist at any time on strict compliance with this License Agreement shall not constitute a waiver of any rights under this License Agreement. This License Agreement shall be construed and governed in accordance with the laws of the State of New York. If any provision of this License Agreement is held to be contrary to law, that provision will be enforced to the maximum extent permissible and the remaining provisions will remain in full force and effect.